HOUSE FLIPPING STRATEGIES

The Ultimate Guide to Create Passive Incomes and Achieve Financial Freedom

Michael Snyder

© Copyright 2020

All rights reserved.

This document is geared towards providing exact and reliable information with regards to the topic and issue covered. The publication is sold with the idea that the publisher is not required to render accounting, officially permitted, or otherwise, qualified services. If advice is necessary, legal or professional, a practiced individual in the profession should be ordered.

From a Declaration of Principles which was accepted and approved equally by a Committee of the American Bar Association and a Committee of Publishers and Associations.

In no way is it legal to reproduce, duplicate, or transmit any part of this document in either electronic means or in printed format. Recording of this publication is strictly prohibited and any storage of this document is not allowed unless with written permission from the publisher. All rights reserved

The information provided herein is stated to be truthful and consistent, in that any liability, in terms of inattention or otherwise, by any usage or abuse of any policies, processes, or directions contained within is the solitary and utter responsibility of the recipient reader. Under no circumstances will any legal responsibility or blame be held against the publisher for any reparation, damages, or monetary loss due to the information herein, either directly or indirectly.

Respective authors own all copyrights not held by the publisher.

The information herein is offered for informational purposes solely, and is universal as so. The presentation of the information is without contract or any type of guarantee assurance.

The trademarks that are used are without any consent, and the publication of the trademark is without permission or backing by the trademark owner. All trademarks and brands within this book are for clarifying purposes only and are the owned by the owners themselves, not affiliated with this document.

Table of Contents

INTRODUCTION 6

MAXIMIZING PROFITS WHEN FLIPPING ASSETS 13

SETTING THE GOALS 15

BASIC STEPS TO FLIP HOUSES FOR PROFIT 17

BENEFITS OF FLIPPING HOUSES 19

THE PEOPLE YOU NEED TO RECRUIT FOR HOUSE FLIPPING. 22

HOUSE FLIPPING BUSINESS STRATEGY 25

RESEARCHING PROPERTY FOR REAL ESTATE INVESTING 28

HOW TO LOCATE POTENTIAL PROPERTIES FOR INVESTMENT IN REAL ESTATE 31

HOW TO FIND PROPERTIES FOR YOUR FIX AND FLIP INITIATIVE 33

HOW TO LOCATE A FREE GOVERNMENT FORECLOSURE LIST 38

HOW TO ASSESS PROPERTIES LIKE A SPECIALIST AND SAVE THOUSANDS OF POUNDS A YEAR? 40

HOW TO PERFORM PROPERTY TITLE SEARCH 46

REAL ESTATE FOR INVESTORS: HOW TO BUY PROPERTY 52

HOW TO REALLY DETERMINE PROPERTY VALUE 56

WHY REAL ESTATE DEVELOPERS AVOID INVESTMENT LOCATION AND TIMING MISTAKES 58

KEY POINTS EVERY REAL ESTATE INVESTOR WILL LEARN BEFORE BUYING FLIP LAND 60

BIGGEST HOME IMPROVING MISTAKES OF REAL ESTATE DEVELOPER 65

HOW TO BUY PROPERTY FOR BACK TAXES AND LESS THAN $200 TO START 67

PREPARING A STEP-BY-STEP REAL ESTATE REVIEW . 69

PREPARE REVIEW 72

HOW SUCCESSFUL INVESTORS PREPARE AN ANALYSIS OF THEIR REAL ESTATE 73

SIX ECONOMIC CRITERIA ON REAL ESTATE VALUATION 79

3 ROOKIE REAL ESTATE ANALYSIS MISTAKES TO AVOID 84

THE BENEFIT OF REAL ESTATE ANALYSIS SOFTWARE 87

ANALYZE YOUR PROSPECTIVE INVESTMENT IN REAL ESTATE FROM TOP TO BOTTOM 90

HOME PRICE-HOW TO NEGOTIATE LIKE A PRO 93

REASONS FOR REJECTION 97

THE SETTING OF THE NEGOTIATIONS 107

HOW TO PLAY A STALE MATE 111

WHAT TO DO WHEN NEGOTIATIONS ARE OVER 113

FINANCING FOR REAL ESTATE INVESTOR 117

- THE 4 TYPES OF IMMOVABLE FINANCING..............122
- REAL ESTATE INVESTING MORTGAGE BROKERS ROLE 130
- HOW TO GET A REAL ESTATE LOAN 132
- GUIDELINES FOR REAL ESTATE INVESTOR REHAB LOAN 135
- THE TOP 'LOAN SHOPPING' REAL ESTATE INVESTOR PITFALLS TO STOP 139
- STRATEGIES TO SURMOUNT CHALLENGES.............142
- REAL ESTATE TEAM 144
- WHY REAL ESTATE ATTORNEY IS THE IMPORTANT MEMBER OF THE REAL ESTATE TEAM? 147
- HOW DO YOU WORK WITH THE BROKERS? 149
- REAL ESTATE: RENEW YOUR PROPERTY.................151
- STARTING A PLAN FOR HOUSE RENOVATION 155
- REAL ESTATE MARKETING TOOLS 157
- CONCLUSION 160

INTRODUCTION

The first thing you need to understand about flipping properties is that it can be more difficult than it sounds. Buying and repairing a rundown house requires a high level of experience and expertise. Of starters, you need to learn how to estimate the cost of fixing windows, constructing a shelter, installing a lock, etc. It's very common for an early investor to underestimate the costs and end up with money lost land. On the other side, you can get going with a less dangerous flip that needs fewer maintenance. For example, if you can get a house that's almost on sale at 30% below market value, you might want to turn it over for some spare cash. The second thing to understand about Hayesville NC and Hiawassee GA real estate flipping is that the money is in the purchase. In other words, how cheap you can purchase a house is usually what determines how much money you're going to make, not how much you can sell it. This is a tried-and-tested principle among real estate investors. Finally, realize that you can play a real estate flipping game at Hayesville NC and Hiawassee GA on a variety of levels. You will make a lot of money to "flip" properties without losing too much financially:

1. You may be a "bird dog" that scans assets for other investors. If you learn how to spot successful flips and find them for customers who really flip them, you might potentially make $500-$1,000 a recommendation without ever spending a dollar of your own.

2. You could have done the option-assignment flips. This includes purchasing a real estate option, seeking a buyer or seller, and "flipping" the property and receiving the difference. You can often make five-digit offers while risking just $5,000-$20,000 as opposed to the full price of the house.

3. You might be a full-fledged real estate flipper. This is the riskiest and most profitable way to get into the real estate flipping game. There are a lot of ways to play the game of flipping real estate, as you can see. There are many risks, but the rewards are also high.

KNOWING THE BASICS OF FLIPPING PROPERTIES

It used to be as simple as buying household goods for resale. Buy-and-sell is the term used for this practice. Today, this is still a form of investment, but it is more of an active business. It's almost like setting up a store to sell things, except that you buy them as if they're going to be part of your personal property. Then, when you feel that their values have been raised, you sell those items. Flipping properties are also about reselling when values have been raised.

WHAT MAKES FLIPPING DIFFERENT?

Flipping properties involve a quick resale of assets with values that may have been raised because of the market or the owner's efforts to improve them. The moves are so fast that the chances of failure and success are higher than any other resale. Of course, if you're very knowledgeable about it, you're looking at very attractive returns. You might be able to compare this fast-moving strategy to scalping in terms of foreign exchange quick strategies. The very name of the tactics says it all: flipping through a page is a matter of quick movement. You've got to get as much information about the asset in as little time as possible so you can get a great deal of value for it.

WHAT KIND OF FLIPPING IS OUT THERE?

Real estate flipping is the most popular thing to do. What you've got to do here is look for homes that can be restored in an appealing, marketable environment. Just go through the repairs. Buyers may be robbed of the prospect of having to make repairs themselves. So, if you don't have a lot of budget riding on this project, you may have to volunteer your own energies. Stay away from dishonest tactics, such as making a house look almost flawless when there are significant hidden issues. Another asset that can be folded is the initial public offering (IPO) of stocks and shares.

Proper knowledge and analysis of the properties you're going to invest in will certainly help you achieve your expected benefit. Get away from dishonest practices. Don't even think about getting embroiled in a flipping mortgage scam. If you're hard-working and well-informed enough, you can make a decent living out of flipping properties-the honest way. Believe it or not, overpricing can actually make you lose out on an investment. If the customers ignore your property because of the frightening price tag, you may pay more for the ads and wait for a longer period to sell your home. You're going to be lucky if you get the overpriced property sold. When your property is stale, you're completely out of touch. You might even have to eat a humble pie and lower the price. Flipping properties is a legitimate investment strategy. With the ability, sound management, and effective budgeting, you will make a healthy profit out of your house. Honest practices still do pay off.

FLIPPING LAND IS A WAY TO MAKE MORE MONEY

Flipping property is a fine way to do real estate business, and this method of dealing with property has gained a great deal of popularity. The term flipping might be a bit confusing to the new entrant in the realtor's career, though it's been around for quite some time now. Online resources that specialize on this topic are structured to provide a large knowledge base on the flipping property industry, and it is advised that someone who is willing to take a foothold in this practice read and review the details presented on the resources. Looking for an appropriate fixing-upper house that you can pick up, renovate, and then sell for a reasonable profit is the usual way for an experienced real estate person to approach a potential business.

The best way to consider a flipping property deal is to calculate the cost of all aspects of an old or "selling" property. Experts are available who can advise you effectively on these issues and make up an evaluation sheet that will show whether or not the arrangement is feasible. If you are not very good at financial calculations in the field of real estate, seek to find a proven real estate agent for this. The word flip property has evoked tremendous interest among those who want to invest some money and turn it around fast. Sometimes they get excited and perform a quick cursory calculation that may not give them the correct solution. Unless you are aware of the current resale value of any house on is" basis, it would be difficult to evaluate and quantify the actual profits that may occur after the flip transaction has been completed and the home resold following renovation. Websites on the Internet may help in this regard, since most investment consultants evaluate real estate deals, taking into account also the idea of flip property turnover and may even notify you of their best estimates for getting the property to the point of a potentially profitable sale. The location of the property you plan to buy for sale must be deliberately selected because the maintenance costs must be relatively small to equate them with the property's selling value before and after maintenance. If you don't do that, you'd be negatively tossing your money rather than flipping property!

THE LUCRATIVE FLIP PROPERTY BUSINESS

Flipping property is considered ingenious by many people who want to make it big in the real estate business or are looking for a quick turnover in the sale of the property as a home business. It's really nothing but financing the renovation of an old property and then selling it for profit. Of course, you need to buy that old property to start with! Considering this as a continuous business is the dream of many people interested in the real estate market. You only need to research the structure and activities that exist in the sector to begin your efforts to make money by turning old houses into new saleable properties. There is a lot of information on the Internet to learn more about this science of turning the property into valued assets. One should research it carefully before jumping into a flipping business.

First and foremost, you must have accounting skills so that you can make the right decisions and return when you consider buying the saleable land, transforming it to one of higher value, and selling it in a profitable manner. Marketing is also a practice that needs to be learned so that the advertising activities are well-created and well-managed. Real estate experts urge the newbie to carefully examine all the pros and cons and their own acumen to start a flip property company. Note that property dedication is a serious thing, and the buyer of your flip deal would want to be confident of what he/she is doing. You will be able to provide all the practical and rational responses to your future client's business queries. It is also necessary to ensure that you are aware of the intricacy of flip deals and know how to calculate the return on investment figures, which are simply an essential part of the business. If you have now decided to enter the flip property sector as an active partner, you will quickly grasp all the rigmaroles of trade and learn the minor ifs and buts before you move into your first flipping deal. There's nothing more exasperating than a botched contract that can destroy your dream and run up huge losses in a monetary way.

MAXIMIZING PROFITS WHEN FLIPPING ASSETS

When you know what you're doing, it's a bit clever on home maintenance and schedule accordingly, it's possible to make a pretty decent amount by flipping properties. One of the effective methods to do this is to rehabilitate homes in need of upgrades or maintenance.

STARTING WITH THE GOVERNMENT AGENCIES

The very best deals when it comes to suitable candidates for selling properties are houses that have been repopulated by drug dealers. Shocking? Maybe that. Because by their very existence, these properties are not the most suitable for the general public, partially because of their location-but mostly because they also need a lot of rehabs. Properties like drug houses and former meth laboratories have seen a lot of neglect and tear, which can be used for an album. This is one of the house flipping tips best suited to those who are skilled at home building and remodeling and have a ready discount hardware supply source because you'll be putting a lot of work into it. However, when it comes to a sheer profit margin, such a property can be ideal for a flipping property.

CHECK THE REAL ESTATE LISTINGS

Granted, rehabilitating the houses used by drug dealers is not for everyone-especially the faint-of-heart or the unskilled. However, it is possible to locate possibilities between foreclosures and land sales; rehabilitating assets like this would possibly take less effort and resources, but if you don't want to spend all your money on the latter, you may also want to focus on a decent retail hardware supplier store.

Although real estate auctions are definitely a source of appropriate assets, we are not endorsing them. The concern is that even though it comes to distressed homes in need of substantial restoration, properties like this are sure to create a lot of interest-and competition when it comes to bidding. One of the most valuable advice for the house is to be mindful of any laws that could prevent you from turning around and selling the house immediately. Of those rehabilitating properties in need of renovation, that is generally not going to be a matter of worry, but you can contact a professional real estate solicitor only on a case-by-case basis.

SETTING THE GOALS

One way to make good money is to lease, renovate, and then sell homes. Known as flipping homes, this activity is very popular in the United States because it offers a great way to make big profits. House flipping as other people call it involves purchasing a home and reselling it to another person. The home is priced for a premium price so that the original seller can make a profit from the sale, and the current owner has the luxury of buying a house free of charge. Most real estate investors are in house flipping because this type of business activity is a perfect way to make money without really investing a lot of money. What buyers typically do is rent a certain property and then seek to find a buyer for it. There is also an evaluation period where the initial buyer may use it to look for a buyer. If and when no purchaser is identified, the original purchaser will still repay the reservation fee and walk away from the property. This is legal in the United States, and it is a common practice to make easy cash without making a big investment.

House flipping involves setting targets as time is essential to actually earning a profit. A land that remains on for too long will no longer be viable even though it is ultimately sold at a lower price. Putting up a timeline for the house renovation is one way to make sure you're on the right track and off to a strong start. This is also necessary to work within the budget and ensure that you don't go overboard and spend above your means. Property purchased at a very low price also requires major repairs. Many real estate investors have suggested that structural improvements are absolutely essential. Ensure your plumbing is perfect, for example, giving you a good reputation as a reliable retailer. You wouldn't want someone to buy a house and then discover that roaches and termites are all over the property. We must always have an excellent reputation as a property investor and a seller. Kitchen and bathroom renovations may be costly, but they certainly add more value to the house. Consider this as a cleaner and better kitchen with granite countertops and will certainly draw more customers in your goals. Improving the bathroom and kitchen tiles will increase the budget a bit, but they're worth the work to boost the place and make a profit. Thus, ensuring that the house's interior is up to the level of living, the exterior of the home must always be very presentable. Although the interior offers warmth, the façade of the house exudes a perfect image for the new owner. Improving the lawn is, therefore, an important part of a house flipping target.

Flipping houses is a perfect way to make money, whether as a full or part-time buyer. Home improvements may not be quick, but when goals are set, they're sure to be enjoyable ventures that produce profits and enjoyment at the end of the day. House flipping is a great project where all parties can be happy as one gets a profit while the other gets a decent place to live in. Start to find a perfect house, set targets, and continue to develop and eventually sell a location for profit.

BASIC STEPS TO FLIP HOUSES FOR PROFIT

The flipping property has received a lot of attention for profit lately. A lot of people have heard of this, but few understand it and the way to go about finding the right properties to flip. Many of you have probably heard of this strategy of flipping houses from watching TV or listening to the radio. If you don't, this book should help you understand the ins and outs of flipping houses and what to look for. Although some people may have had negative experiences with this money-making strategy because of bad deals or less than perfect work done by shady contractors, by following the advice here, you'll be flipping the right way to make a profit and avoiding all the negative aspects by having your heads up on what to look for. One of the most important aspects of cashing on the real estate flipping market is choosing an appropriate location. You've certainly heard this a lot of times before, but it couldn't be any further from the fact that location is the single most important aspect of value assessment in any real estate. In order to make a flip, a good house needs to be in a desirable location. It's good to check the local newspapers in your area for houses that move relatively well in a specific neighborhood. This will assist you in finding the successful flipping property downwards.

Besides choosing a good venue, it is also necessary to search at properties that require only slight improvements and minimal cosmetic touches to suit them. This is very important because you don't want to tie up valuable money and time to renovate a property. When you're bound to one property because of the amount of maintenance that needs to be done on it, you're more likely to lose income. This is where you can be wise and order a home inspection. The sum of money expended on a successful home inspection will most likely pay off later and will save you a lot in time and energy. The inspection can uncover hidden problems within the property and allow you to adjust your bid to cover the cost of repairs.

Finding a good contractor can easily make or break a deal. It is very important to communicate directly with your contractor as time is of the essence when flipping a property for profit. Look for a contractor that has a good reputation and is familiar with this type of work. Ask around at your local real estate offices about various contractors. Real estate agents can be a great source of information. Once you've found a trustworthy contractor, it is important to relay your needs concerning timeliness and workmanship. Being upfront and knowing what to expect from one another is a key facet of a successful business relationship.

Flipping houses can be a very profitable venture if done correctly and with the proper knowledge. Getting past the above basic steps is a must in order to be successful in this business. You'll need to have everything in order and a sharp mind ready to do some negotiating for the best deals. Operating well with a partner, keeping a positive outlook, and being well versed in basic house flipping skills is a must. If you focus on the important advice included here and apply this knowledge, you will be an expert in no time and be rewarded earnestly.

BENEFITS OF FLIPPING HOUSES

Of course, the most obvious benefit of flipping houses is the potentially big capital gain that can be made. There are, though, a few other, more theoretical incentives you need to be mindful of when you start on flipping houses to attain your real estate capital. There are also pros and cons involved with the flipping homes, as in other aspects of life. By flipping houses, many lessons can be learned; the skills and information you'll acquire will certainly be applied in many other life circumstances.

Budgeting-There are really not many things that can teach you how to budget as quickly as flipping houses. While flipping a house, you'll need to know/learn how to budget quickly or lose a lot of money. Two very important skills for house flipping are establishing a budget and sticking to it. Once you've learned this talent, you'll be surprised by how many possibilities will pop out in other aspects of life.

Muscle Definition-You can see that house flipping can be a very good exercise. This is very true for those people who do most of the work themselves (this is recommended if you want to cut back those expensive, profit-taking labor costs).

Attention to detail-This capability will be enhanced every time you flip a house. When flipping houses, small things will make a big difference. The key is not to overlook small things like proper staging, electrical faceplates, and a good eye for color throughout the property. It's very critical that the customer views the property as a place they've been cared for, rather than seeing it as just another spot on their list they've got to see today. This is a value that can be used in all areas of life. You're going to start looking differently at everything from your partnership to tax preparation.

Positive Thinking - You've probably heard many times about how important positive thinking is to many people. This is very true of the house flipping. It's always good to add a little realism to your positive thinking once in a while, but you should be mindful that positive thinking is very effective in flipping houses and most other aspects of life. Someone once said, "Everything in life is easy when you're optimistic; it's hard to be positive every day."

Just do it- If flipping houses were to teach you only one thing, it would be this. Every day that you own the house, you pay for it (mortgage, interest, etc.). After you launch, everything is simpler. Instead of thinking about all the stuff that could go wrong, just do something about it and don't think or talk about it.

Often, being able to measure the worth of the property is helpful. This comes with a mix of market analysis and practice. Walk around your neighborhood and take a look at all the signs for sale. Take the newspaper and start seeing what the houses are going to do. Once you've got the feeling of what a house is worth, you'll be surprised at how many good opportunities they 're starting to see. And as you improve this skill, there are more opportunities.

Flipping houses isn't rocket science, but making a profit in this particular industry takes a rare mix of talent, skill, and stubbornness. Following the above lessons would help you excel not only when it comes to flipping houses but also in other facets of your life. Even though flipping houses isn't the hardest thing in the world, it takes a unique combination of skills, luck, research, and stubbornness to make a profit. Learning the above-mentioned skills, you are guaranteed success in flipping houses and in life. You'll find that all the work, commitment, and money is just a small price to pay for the knowledge and experience you 're going to get.

THE PEOPLE YOU NEED TO RECRUIT FOR HOUSE FLIPPING.

A couple of years ago, house flipping became a big business. It was so big that there were more than five reality shows on house flipping, and these shows were highly rated. House flipping is still a very profitable real estate company that you can get into if you have enough money. House flipping is basically buying an abandoned house, renovating it and selling it at a good price. If you're interested in getting into a house flipping company, you need to know the people you need to recruit to support you from start to finish.

1. A trustworthy architect

Architects may be notorious as house designers, but they are also excellent at testing the building's condition – whether it is well-built, solid, and whether you can alter parts of the house without losing stability. Including an architect in your team is a benefit for your flipping company, because some of your rivals may not have their own architects. Select an architect who has a strong reputation who is willing to do a job depending on the budget.

2. A good interior designer and decorator.

Selling a house is challenging because the interior is not well-designed. Therefore you possibly should recruit an interior designer. Interior designers are creators whose canvas makes up the buildings' interior. They will help you choose the right color to paint the walls, put the furniture and decorations to make the house appealing to prospective buyers. To prevent disputes about the look of the home interior, make sure the interior designer you prefer is someone you are comfortable with who has the same style as you do when it comes to decoration.

3. The Fast Renovation Company

When picking a construction firm to do the real house maintenance and remodeling you 're turning over, you have to make sure they have sufficiently skilled staff who can work fast so you can get a strong return on your investment. Remember, you've got competitors in this business too, and if they finish their home faster than you do, they can steal away your potential client. But don't sacrifice quality for speed, or else no one will trust you again. Remember, a renovation company with high-quality, efficient builders is what you want.

4. Real estate brokers

It is optional to get a real estate broker, but it is recommended. Real estate brokers have the experience to spot prospective clients, as well as connections who will help them identify customers who are searching for properties. The real estate broker you chose should be someone you can trust, and this person should have no previous or current interest in any conflict. You should check at your area for a directory of real estate brokers approved for this work. House flipping is lucrative, especially if you have the proper personnel on your team. The list above will help lead you in seeking and selecting trustworthy teammates on your journey to make house flipping money.

HOUSE FLIPPING BUSINESS STRATEGY

The house flipping cycle can be divided into three phases: home acquisition, home renovation, and home selling. Every process is essential and special, and each process must draw on the strengths and weaknesses of the previous phases.

Phase One: Home Purchase

Each phase is the most critical process as it sets the stage for the remainder of the house flipping project. If you choose the wrong house to sell, you will be forced to pay higher than expected construction costs and be forced to deal with a longer period than expected. On the other hand, if you choose the right house, the building and selling process will practically take care of itself. Many real estate experts believe that you don't make money from the flipped home sale, but from the acquisition of the property. You always want to keep an end in mind. The end of the house flipping would be to make money. Therefore, choosing the right house to fit your budget and your schedule means that you'll have a very easy time renovating and selling your house.

Phase Two: House renovation work

The best approach to implement to ensure a good house flip is to set your budget and plan before you start constructing. With a budget and timeline plan, you'll know how much time you will spend on your flip, as well as how long the flip will take. You can better track your progress in this way. For construction, the three most important considerations for the production of the final product are time, money, and price. All three of these variables are interrelated. For example, if you want to speed up the construction process, it will cost you more money, and the quality of the work will be affected, most definitely adversely. If you're trying to install the finest quality technology in your house, it'll probably cost you more time and more money. Ultimately, if you want to spend as little money as possible, expect the quality to suffer and the project's duration to last longer.

Phase Three: House Selling

Depending on how well you've surveyed your target market and what kind of changes you've added to your flip in the previous phases, the home sales process will last only a few weeks. Anything longer than a month, you will be forced to pay for an additional mortgage payment that will reduce your overall profits. To ensure that you quickly sell a flipped house, you should follow these two guides: set your selling price below the market value and market your home. The name of the game in house flipping is pace, and when you put the house's selling price below the market average, potential homebuyers will see the added benefits of your renovation relative to your lower asking price and will automatically see a huge value. To order to increase foot traffic in your neighborhood, authorizing a real estate agent to advertise your home on the Multiple Listing Service (MLS) would allow even more real estate agents to showcase your property. Also, the more potential homebuyers you can look at your house, the more likely someone is to like it and ultimately buy a flipped house. There is no one right way to flip a house. Many forms, though, are dramatically greater than others. What works with some of the projects might not work with others. Determine your budget and timetable, and still have an end target in mind from the start. If you can do that effectively, you 're well on your way to a profitable house flipping project.

RESEARCHING PROPERTY FOR REAL ESTATE INVESTING

Much has been written about spending lately. Other investments may be made. Credit Union Rate is the source of market knowledge and investment potential. It is worth noting that there is no safe investment and that all investment is at risk. However, investment in real estate tends to be less risky, as most property values go up rather than down. And even when interest rates are in transition, the average value of real estate tends to increase. It's a brilliant idea to talk to your credit union financial advisor about current trends in your area and how real estate investment can diversify your portfolio. But information is needed just like any good investor to make a wise investment decision. You ought to have a decent concept of what you are investing in and their potential. Blind investment is a good way to lose rather than make money. Here are some tips for more effective real estate analysis with investment potential.

Well, understand the neighborhood. Study a neighborhood thoroughly before buying a property there. Know that for starter homes, any of the young people live in there. These neighborhoods frequently see turnover as families grow, and young couples improve. You need to learn about the key residents of the region to know how to properly sell land. Is the neighborhood safe? And, of course, how's the location? It is considered much more attractive if the area is near a good college, minutes away from shopping, and away from the major thoroughfares.

Determine the future prospects of the region. Like the previous tip, it is important to know whether the area has growth potential. The area that is run down and expected to be destroyed to make way for a new highway or service station is not a sound investment. Nonetheless, if a developer is planning to open high-end retail, eating, and entertainment plaza a few blocks away, you're likely to find that the area has great potential for growth. If you want to buy land, check to see if the city's growth rate warrants you buying a few acres on edge, allowing you to hold it until the developers need it to expand.

Look out for new developments. Keep an eye on newspapers and town council sessions. This will give you a "pass" on where the best places are situated. Beautification projects are great things to keep in mind in "rundown" areas since they usually mean money inflows and new attractions. However, make sure the contractor is reliable; otherwise, you may notice that you've been swept up with the majority of the inhabitants of the community when glitches, controversies, and stoppages are all part of the scheme.

Don't forget about the Internet. The Internet is a perfect way to search for future real estate investment opportunities. Your range immediately extends beyond your immediate locality. You can actually seek out opportunities across the country or from the other side of the world. But, as with all things on the Internet, you 're supposed to be careful. The Internet is also a prime location for scam artists to find unwitting victims.

As with all investments, something that seems "too good to be true" is important to avoid. Real estate investment is not about making "easy money." Whether you're planning to invest by owning and then using the house for a few years before selling or planning to rent or lease the land to someone else, real estate investment can be a profitable proposition. You will be sure to make the most use of your investment dollar by conducting extensive work before you make a purchase.

HOW TO LOCATE POTENTIAL PROPERTIES FOR INVESTMENT IN REAL ESTATE

Real estate is perhaps the most secure and risk-free path to capital for most of us, but a very important part of investing is learning how to locate the best assets. Knowing this can help you have a successful real estate investment career. The natural choice of investment properties is close to home unless you live in a depressed area. The only time you can invest in a depressed area is when you have information that indicates that the area will soon turn around. In that case, it could be the best choice for you. Why is the best choice in the vicinity of your home? If you spend close to where you live, it makes it much easier for you to review your property, renters, the progress of renovations, and develop relationships with real estate agents and contractors who can support you.

You also need to consider your financial situation. Can you afford to hire a management company to raise rentals to keep your investment going? If you're going to have to do this yourself, the closest you get to home, the better. Can you afford to fly out and check your properties? If not, the closer you get to your home, the better. Would driving an hour each way to service each property take too large a chunk of your time and gas? If the answer is yes, the closer to home, the better. This is the question more people ask: is owning a foreclosed property a decent future investment?

Foreclosures may or may not always be a bargain. There are, however, negotiations out there, and in many cases, they are foreclosures. You can find foreclosed properties through a realtor who specializes in them or through a local foreclosure database, either online or in print. Many banks are selling their foreclosures, and some are listing them with realtors.

HOW TO FIND PROPERTIES FOR YOUR FIX AND FLIP INITIATIVE

If you're going to fix and sell houses for a living, it's a great time to do that. Due to the recent housing bubble and the global economic recession, real estate prices are generally low. You can buy large investment assets in many parts of the country without having to dig further into your pockets. Any people might think that real estate investors are now happier than their predecessors because they have convenient access to affordable homes that they can rehabilitate. Nonetheless, this will not always be the case because rehabbers can't locate investment property. Finding the right house, you 're going to repair and sell isn't that easy. According to experienced rehabbers, much of the time devoted to rehabilitating a house is expended on the site of productive assets. And if you're looking to renovate your upper room, you 're going to need a lot of time. But to make life a bit simpler for you, here are some tips on locating assets that you can rehabilitate:

· Attend public auctions or search out local banks to see if they are selling property. Lending firms will be decent sources of investment property because many households lose their homes because of their failure to pay their mortgages due to foreclosures. Because of the current financial downturn, these borrowers are having difficulty financing all of these assets. They are therefore prepared to sell those homes at prices below their market value.

· Speaking to inspired home sellers. Due to the economic crisis, there has been an increase in the number of homeowners who want to quickly sell their properties. Motivated home sellers can provide you with affordable investment properties. These people don't usually ask for a higher selling price. As long as you help them get rid of their unwanted properties at the soonest possible time, they will consider your offer.

· Use bird dogs to find properties that you can fix and flip. For a small fee, you can ask bird dogs to find you profitable houses. By using other people's talents, you can save a lot of time and money.

· Move around the neighborhood. Surprisingly enough, many rehabbers found nice fixer-upper homes just by driving around a particular place. So, if you're going to use this particular strategy, don't forget to look for vacant houses because they can bring you big profits.

FLIP PROPERTIES TO BEWARE WHEN BUYING

Flipping property soon becomes one of the most lucrative ways of investing in real estate for a fast and efficient investment return. You will undoubtedly find a flip to beware of, and as in any business, a sound real estate investor will instinctively recognize when to flip a property and when not to flip it. For those who have yet to gain insight into the business, look at the warning signs early before going to any deal.

GOOD REASONS WHY YOU NEED TO RECONSIDER

1. A wide range of plumbing problems – plumbing systems are extremely expensive, not to mention time-consuming, requiring a licensed person to carry out inspections by local building inspectors. In all cases, if there is a lot of plumbing work to be done, the property is definitely not worth the trouble, regardless of how a house appeals to you unless it is an absolute steal.

2. Repairs to the roof can be required, but the total replacement of the roof and its insulation is out of the question and should be avoided at all costs. However, in most situations, considered a major investment. The exception to this law can be beneficial if you have a return on your investment that more than doubles, having the house in an appropriate location. Avoid making extensive renovations at all costs because you know the market and can benefit from such a big substitution.

3. The floors are one of the most significant features of any house, and probably the most attractive sales attribute to a prospective purchaser. If the floors need less attention in terms of carpet and linoleum cleaning, you may be in a good position to take care of these items, but if the structural part of the floor is so bad that it requires a total replacement, then it is a wise decision

to cancel the deal as it would take a considerable amount of money to bring the property within the market value range.

4. The location of the house is a major concern, and no matter how attractive the property is, if it is located in a demographic area that is not suitable for prospective buyers, it will take a much longer time to sell. It's best to avoid chasing good money after bad in such properties and eventually become a burden anchor.

5. The availability of basic amenities such as airports, shopping centers, supermarkets, schools, and hospitals should all be within easy reach. Houses that are too far away from the conveniences that people have become used to will be hard to sell for rent.

6. Kitchen and bathroom remodels are a very attractive feature for prospective home buyers. In almost all situations, investments in the kitchen will return three or five times more to your money. The exception to this rule would be determined by factors such as the location of the house, the neighborhood, the house's size, and the right type, which would quickly turn around because such costs could be high.

7. If the property is a foreclosure and the bank is willing to finance it, this means that the property is more than likely to be a hot item, so that the deal can be finalized for all practical reasons. However, if you notice that the financial institution is reluctant or hesitant to finance, it's the best idea to make the deal.

8. Sometimes it is possible to purchase houses that have been on the market for a very long time at a very low price, and sometimes you can turn a strong home into a dream home. Always look at why the property is not being sold in a timely manner, because although the inside of the house may be a perfect picture, there may be other problems that are not so obvious on the outside.

9. You 're going to find that some of the sellers are in a big hurry to finalize the sale so they can move on and do it. This is the most appropriate time to negotiate a reduced price, and it is where you can make great deals with substantial profits. You've got it in a nutshell. Note that you're not going to stay in the home and that you're just there to hand over the land to make a profit, so make changes and market easily accordingly. If you're a helpful person when it comes to maintenance, you 're going to benefit even more, but there's going to be a moment when making deals on properties and arranging is going to be the primary concern for success.

HOW TO LOCATE A FREE GOVERNMENT FORECLOSURE LIST

Place of a free government foreclosure listing is not as complicated as it seems. Such collections can only be accessed somewhere online. A government foreclosure listing usually sells homes but also sells a variety of other items. Motor homes, refurbished cars, and other tangible items are sold to the government at federal auctions. A free government foreclosure listing will allow anyone to find a government foreclosure piece of property. Although they are sold cheaply, they are usually sold at auctions both online and in a designated area. These listings help anyone to locate properties in distress. Such properties are usually repositioned for one purpose or another. They 're sold to get money back missing in the auction, and in some cases, they've been absolutely robbed of everything. We are sold "as they are," and the customer takes full responsibility for them. Extensive repairs may be required, up to and including full restorations.

By finding a free foreclosure listing, you can easily find a property in your area that might be worth buying. They are published online as well as in daily newspapers. Finding one of these properties can be a big deal for a smart investor who buys and sells properties for profit. Investors know how to use capital to buy and sell easily, and to sell such assets makes them very effective. By using these types of listings, they can buy and sell real estate with the term "flipping" one after the other. Every type of business is used solely to generate cash flow. The investor wins, the home is fixed, which in turn may increase the value of the property in the area. It's a win-win situation, and it all starts with finding the right free government foreclosure listing. By the way, by studying and analyzing the Best Free Foreclosure Listings services on the market, you would be able to decide which one fits the particular criteria, plus free or discounted alternatives. This way, you'll save time through up-to-date foreclosure listings and money by getting better results over your investment.

HOW TO ASSESS PROPERTIES LIKE A SPECIALIST AND SAVE THOUSANDS OF POUNDS A YEAR?

The art of correctly surveying land is a talent that many landowners and developers should have given their right arm to master. For a qualified owner, one of the irritating little costs that you still have to pay is the land survey. Wouldn't it be nice to reduce the number of in-depth surveys you have to pay for per year? The post would go into more depth about how to test the land yourself. It's going to send you a checklist of important items to watch out for when you're looking at properties. At the conclusion of this, you should have enough information to be able to make educated decisions about the status of any given land. The first thing you need to do is to make sure you're ready. Below is a rundown of a few things you might want to take with you when you see a possible investment property.

Camera/Video camera

Pen

Notepad

Voice memo

Binoculars

Any descriptions of the property you already have from the estate agent, the Internet, the seller, or any other way. A useful tip (though not always practical) is to try and do a survey in wet conditions. That way, you can see issues with fallen drains, leaky roofs, defective guttering, or any other damp or rain-related problems. You don't actually have to do the survey in the order specified. Nonetheless, it might be wise to start by taking a walk around the property and trying to get a general feeling for it and the place.

External Roof

What's is it made of?

Check the ceiling of the room below the loft for signs of damage to the water or any other problems that may have arisen as a result of a roof problem.

What is the general repair state of the roofs? Be sure to look at the roof from all angles, as often difficulties can only be seen from a certain direction.

Take a look at the Chimney Stack. Check for signs of loss of brick or damage. This is where the binoculars might be handy.

External Walls

What kind of construction are the exterior walls, i.e., solid brick, stone, or something else?

Is the pointing all right? What kind of finish is on the walls? Is that a pebble dash, a stone, brick, or something else? Sometimes the finish that has been used will help to determine the age of the property.

Look out for bulges on the wall or signs of moisture or staining.

Look for cracks or signs of movement around the corners of doors or window frames. When you notice flaws in these places, it may be a precursor to more severe issues. When you find something that looks unusual, take a look at the other property on the street and see if they have a similar problem. Special notice of any cracks below the damp proof level can suggest significant property problems.

Out Buildings

Check the state of any property-related to the outbuildings that include sheds, garages, outside offices, barns, stables, toilets, or anything else.

Modifications

Check the status of any changes made to the house. Check additions, loft conversions, basement conversions (be highly aware of any issues with damp conversions in the basement, since these conversions are infamous for damp problems, if not correctly built). You must review the applicable documents to ensure that things have been completed in compliance with the construction laws and that planning permission has been secured. It is also a good idea to see any current guarantees or warranties the vendor has.

Internal

Is the property modern, existing (older), or renovated?

What is the general state of repair of the interior of the property? Did it seem to have been well looked after?

Is there something the decoration is trying to hide? Hold in mind the ceilings finished in a dark color that could conceal any hidden secrets, such as water loss, beneath the paintwork.

Is there some form of sound insulation in the ceiling, floors, or walls?

Does the property have original features that will add to its value?

What's the Windows state, and what's it made of? Were the windows double-glazed? Will they look like they need to be removed or repaired? Windows in disrepair can be perfect for helping you secure a better price with the retailer.

There's a moist proof test. Often you can say this by inspecting the walls outside the house. When there is a black line between two to three bricks high, that could probably mean that a moist proof course is present.

Other things to check

When you're trying to be diligent with your property analysis, you'll definitely want to test the seven points in the list below.

What is the state of the fixtures and fittings in the property?

Was there a central heating system? How old is the cooker? Are there documents available to display the history of the service?

Is there a shared main water source and a water meter which has been installed?

Check for adequate ventilation in the house, particularly in areas such as kitchens and bathrooms.

Is there a kind of trip system for the electrical supply? How old is that? Does it look like it will need to be replaced or restored in the near future?

Attempt to search behind any furniture or equipment that is out of place. They might have been put there to hide a question lurking behind them.

You will flush the toilets and run the water to ensure if the water is drained properly and to ensure that there are no unusual sounds, such as a sudden knock while the bath is flowing.

Ultimately, do not hesitate to search the property register and find out the exact price that similar properties in the city have recently sold. There are a lot of free websites on the Internet that you can get this information from.

All of the items listed above can be checked and verified by you as well as by a surveyor who goes to property and walks around it for 25 minutes. Knowing how to assess land yourself is not really something you need to be able to do. Nonetheless, if you have a contractor with whom you work on a regular basis or a relative, then it's better you to try and drag him to visit your property-especially the first few-until you gain more confidence. The truth is, most surveyors are not very busy with their day-to-day jobs, and the skills they use to do the normal run of the mill property survey cover only a fraction of what they spent years learning.

HOW TO PERFORM PROPERTY TITLE SEARCH

It is not a long ago when performing property title search was a very hectic and tiring job. Not only did it absorb time and resources, but it also consumed a very significant amount of capital. Imagine for a second that you do have to spend too many sums on home sales and prices, but before you buy, you have to pay a very good sum of money to the land broker. Until the advent of development and industrialization, land maintenance was perceived to be the most difficult work to do. This is known that land titles are not found near your home, so there were no reliable transit facilities available in the early days, so it was a very difficult job to look for properties and move from one location to another. Often, the Internet wasn't there for Google stuff. People used to rely heavily on real estate dealers and managers to buy properties. Most of the time, people have been cheated by land sellers. Some situations in which people have been good have had too many issues. Then the question emerges, how do you conduct the land title search? Fortunately, we are living in a new age, and the Internet has already overcome much of our tough tasks. Below are certain things to keep in mind when looking for title property successfully. If you are purchasing a home, you also need to check for specific legal documentation and information about the land. They must also cross-check these records with the municipal authority for any fault or theft, etc. Upon acceptable results, it's your turn to dig closely at the property you 're looking to purchase. Another of the tools is the Internet. To that end, you need to open a search engine like Google, Yahoo, or Bing and investigate the identity of the owner of the property and then cross-check for other names that may or may not exist with the house, such as witnesses and legal authority, etc.

There may be a lot of ways to conduct title search properties, but you need to find the ones that best suit you. You ought to be 100 % confident that the land is free from any dispute if it appears when the land is being sold to two or three individuals at a time and is the main challenge. Each of them argues the property is his own, and this dispute takes all to justice. It's easier to look into problem situations where they occur. Tour the property in person at least two or three times. Tell your neighbors and people about the house. There may be ghost incidents and property that can cause significant complications later, so be mindful of them as well. Just be 100% assured that these things are not connected to the properties and that all is good. It would be smart to investigate the location and surroundings of your house, bus stops, markets, car parks, playgrounds, etc. When you've been pleased with all of the above, it's time to learn the house price. How are you going to get an understanding of the actual price of the property? To do so, you need to contact the municipal authority in the area who will direct you to the city's real rates. Why ask them, as they have all the details about the properties that are being sold in the area. That would improve your expertise, and that is how you can do land title check very quickly and effectively.

HOW CAN YOU PURCHASE A PROPERTY AND FLIP IT?

Investing in real estate is a very rewarding practice. It's not just a refuge for you and your mates. It also is part of your income, thereby growing your financial capability in the eyes of borrowers and sellers. Apart from these benefits, you might also use your investment as a way of producing more profits. Through purchasing a property and selling it, you can sell it at a price that will give your finances the boost they need. If you want to know more about how to purchase an inexpensive property and sell it afterward, you should read it.

Which kind of property would you buy?

You may also buy other kinds of real estate property at a low price. Nonetheless, the best real estate prices are obtained by purchasing a foreclosed home or a struggling homeowner's property. They usually have rock-bottom rates, but you could sell them for a better valuation after you've managed to upgrade it and make it look as good as fresh. It is important to note, though, that purchasing a mortgage or property owned by a financially distressed vendor still has its risks. You will battle these risks by performing a comprehensive home review before you finalize your order. That way, you might quantify the various expenses that you might need to spend in order to restore and upgrade it, and equate that with the amount of income that you could hypothetically gain by selling that.

How would you fund your investment and the requirements for improvement?

You will also look for a good funding alternative that you can use before buying a home. The money you would benefit from it will be used to pay for your investment and the expense of increasing its esthetic performance. While considering a lending option, you may either apply for a mortgage or employ a professional loan officer. Applying for a mortgage means that you have to negotiate with a financial agency or trust. They typically offer loans that are equal to 80% of the amount of the order. Therefore, you will also need to find a way to fund the remaining 20% and the improvements that the property would require. In the meantime, a professional loan officer might search for a lending alternative that will finance 100 percent of the house's valuation, as well as the different home renovation measures that you might need to conduct. Such circumstances illustrate that recruiting a loan officer is always a better choice than buying a mortgage from a bank or a lending agency.

Which is the most productive way to sell it?

You'll still need to develop new campaign strategies and approaches to effectively sell your home. That way, more clients will be able to make higher offers for your house. Apart from these marketing tactics, you will still need to stop staging your house until the necessary maintenance and home renovation procedures have been completed. In doing so, the customers will not be able to see the former status of the house you're trying to sell. Just note these three things when you're trying to sell the property you've bought at a reasonable price. If you find these ideas, you can never fail to achieve your target of producing more profits.

REAL ESTATE FOR INVESTORS: HOW TO BUY PROPERTY

Real estate to clients is potentially the most valuable part of the business when it comes to being a property flipper. It's the soul, the blood of your business. But, as real estate owners, we can't simply buy any property that anyone presents to us. Although it might sound nice to come out of someone's lips, we need to believe, but still, test, and if the numbers don't make sense, we need to have the confidence to get away from the offer. Mind that when you order, you make money as a flipper. With that being said, buying an investment property requires skills. It's like learning how to ride a bike for the first time. Yes, it's going to be a little frightening at first, but once you get the hang of it, you may be able to do it with your eyes closed. There's a formula that all investors follow to purchase deals that make sure you make money when you buy. It's known as the 70's law.

What's the 70's rule? The 70's law is essentially operating like this. Let's just presume you find a house worth $100k ARV-(After Repair Value) The highest amount you would expect to pay for this house should be $70k. (Very easy math) Take $100,000 ARV and multiply it by.70 or 70 percent, which is equivalent to $70,000. If you buy real estate as an owner at 70 percent or below the FMV (Fair Market Value), you offer a safety net of 30 percent. Generally, if you've done your homework right, you will pocket 20 percent of it as a bonus, which is $20,000 and 10 percent for your closing costs. How about if the property needs to be repaired? Unless the land is a house in trouble, what you have to do is follow the same formula: 70 minus repairs. As buyers, this is vital to your growth, and you will potentially find offers for less than 70 in today's real estate markets. You could potentially pick up offers for as little as 30 to 50 cents on the dollar. The deals are out there; you just need to know when and how to find them. By sticking to the 70-principle rule for flipping properties, you would never have a problem making money. Note, investment property requires diligence, patience, and good schooling.

KNOW HOW ESTATE AGENTS VALUE PROPERTIES FOR SALE

Each homeowner would like to sell his or her property for its full worth. However, too many, they end up picking an estate agent purely on the basis of the person who offers them the best initial valuation. However, this is going to be an expensive mistake. What your house is priced for. When you have the calculation incorrect, it may be priced at a price less than the real valuation of the land. On the other hand, even overpriced houses will drive prospective buyers away from seeing your home. Moreover, high sales rates can also lead to a long delay before any decent bid comes in or may not be offered at all. It is therefore recommended to get the valuation done by the right agent.

Few Considerations Estate Agents Keep in Mind When Valuing Land

1. Local Amenities

During the property valuation, one of the main factors that can drive up the selling price is the area where the house is located. Aspects such as how close the house is to schools, shopping centers, banks, restaurants, and parks certainly affect the final sale price. A home with good transport links will get a much better price than a house located in a secluded location.

2. Scale

When it comes to having your house priced, the size of your home is another important thing that estate agents bear in mind. The number of bedrooms that the house has had an effect on the selling of the land. Also, the scale of each space is primarily dictated by the ethnicity of the buyer.

3. Aesthetics

Besides the obvious reasons, such as keeping your house well kept, tidy, and safe, few other architectural aspects can help you maximize your home's value. Properties that offer fantastic views or are near to water sources should also have a higher sales price. Even as hotel rooms with scenic views cost higher, so do houses by the river or the sea.

4. Kerby's Attraction

Estate agents agree that the way the property appears from the outside is as critical as the inside. Upon checking at the house, the agent will decide whether the front garden looks tidy and well-tended and whether your house stands out from the others. A house with broad exteriors is guaranteed to get a better deal than one that doesn't have.

5. Potentials

While the house scale plays a critical role in the valuation of the land, the residence's versatility is always measured. Agents also search to see if a single property can be expanded. A house with the ability to be changed will help a lot with the sale price. Properties with room for enhancement and restoration will push up selling prices dramatically.

HOW TO REALLY DETERMINE PROPERTY VALUE

For others who are eager or inspired to sell their home, the right first thing to ask is: are you able to purchase the house at the price you're selling it? This provides a very good idea of the price they set. First, they ask their neighbors after a long time if they will purchase the property for the price it is being paid. That alone will give you a clear understanding of the value of the land. Neighbors should include details as to whether or why they will not buy the property at a date. What is important to others is the city and its surrounding communities. Normally, a decent neighborhood is better valued than a high-end suburb with vast property perceived to be occupied by corrupt individuals! Remember the interests of those involved in purchasing a property. If there is a nice, accurate sample of choice data, try to get a copy of it. There are those who like the woods or the suburbs, and others find it best close or inside the business districts. No matter how cheap a property is, if no one likes it, it has no value at all! For e.g., you have a very close friend or customer who wants to purchase inexpensive big plots of land and hold on to it, so you have a buyer that only a few will have. Yeah, you know his choice. With this, determining property value for that buyer has its set parameters. It's going to be a straightforward matter of understanding the local property market prices that you want to invest in. Twit or without structures is not a concern here. Home properties also have a norm for evaluating land prices. Current market valuation, recent transactions in the area, accredited evaluation, and comparative business research are typical strategies. It is necessary to know the style of building and materials used in the house or structure itself. Understanding it would provide a reasonable idea of how much it will cost per square foot to build a home. Remember the age of the building; as for older ones, any depreciation would have to be removed from the period it was constructed.

Note that there are a lot of magnificent and well-built houses in the wrong place. We are also priced high for the structure but not for the worth of the property. It could also have high-tech services and protections because of a poor neighborhood! Therefore, the calculation of the worth of property such as these should not be approached in the traditional manner. Use common sense and logic to test the true value properties of this kind. The calculation of the real interest of the mortgaged assets can be viewed from a particular perspective. Do not find the interest paid as part of the benefit. If ever, consider only the potential interest, whether it is fair or not for evaluation. Real estate investors should only consider the value that the property has and should be returned within a short period of time.

WHY REAL ESTATE DEVELOPERS AVOID INVESTMENT LOCATION AND TIMING MISTAKES

In order to excel in trading, a real estate developer must have a good grasp of the idea of position and timing. Since future investments often consist of a wide range of options that investors need to narrow down to position (i.e., where and when to make an investment and timing). As a result, they are studying the market in order to find a specific property located in a particular neighborhood, town or region that provides the most value and to invest at a time when market conditions allow them to buy low and sell high (and certainly not when prices have peaked and resulted in the opposite effect). Nevertheless, this is not as direct as it sounds and does enable an investor to learn how to filter and apply specific data in a manner that helps them to differentiate between what is valid and what is important to their investment purpose and what is not. Take, for example, the comparative statistics on real estate developments published by the U.S. Census Bureau and the National Association of Realtors. Although supplying investors with incredibly useful knowledge on average developments for the country as a whole, they do not define consumer supply and demand for investment property in any single region. In other words, if the buyer is not diligent in paying close attention to and evaluating local market trends, he or she could make the mistake of timing a decision to purchase an investment property based on a predictor that appears to be more subjective than true.

Therefore, it is necessary for investors to find the data applicable to the particular category of rental property that is being pursued. For instance., if you want to buy an apartment building, you don't want to make an investment decision based on local developments in raw land or commercial buildings. In this situation, you want to focus your decision on costs, leases, occupancy, and demand for comparable other apartment buildings. It always makes sense to monitor local trends, but bear in mind that these various types of real estate never move in the same direction, and any pattern that might have an effect on one's valuation could be totally irrelevant to the value of others. In the same way, investors in real estate must also differentiate between supply and demand patterns for different real estate types. For e.g., high rental demand for a single-family home will not imply a strong rental demand for an apartment complex; or lower-than-average occupancy for a three-bedroom two-bath unit encourages lower occupancy rates for certain unit configurations. Therefore, when you are attempting to assess the value of a property for an investment decision, do not mistake one method of supply and demand with another; always pay particular attention to the patterns in supply and demand that are most important to the nature and structure of real estate you are dealing with.

Okay, so the issue of where and when to buy a rental property will also depend on

an analysis of market patterns in your immediate region,

the application of data that is unique to a particular category of property, and

the ability to differentiate one source of supply and demand from another.

Sure, investing in real estate is rarely easy, and definitely does not guarantee wealth and prosperity. But real estate owners, who base their investment choices on a meticulous review and analysis of both position and timing factors, routinely discover the opportunity for gains.

KEY POINTS EVERY REAL ESTATE INVESTOR WILL LEARN BEFORE BUYING FLIP LAND.

It doesn't matter whether you've been buying properties to sell profitably for decades or whether you're just starting out, it's still useful to look at some of the core aspects of how you handle yourself and your company. This is particularly important if you run your investment company in a small or medium-sized market. Why? Since your credibility is always going to keep you alive. You may think you're doing just fine, but if other real estate professionals in your industry have various opinions of you and your company, you might well be losing your company-and your money. Here are a few key points to keep in mind when you do your business.

Take your feelings out of the equation.

The first thing to consider when buying properties is to distinguish the sentimental, family side from the business side. You may love the property and be excited about putting the offer together, but purchasing it from a commercial perspective does not make sense. Perhaps the numbers just don't make any sense, so you're expected to take a miss, so keep trying. People will also have trouble distinguishing what they're passionate about and what they want from what falls into their business model.

Need to be constructive.

It's clearly a positive idea to be motivated and have a love for what you're doing. It is particularly important when you get through the day-to-day challenges of trying to pull a contract done when things don't go the way you want to. That's why it's really important to be upbeat and optimistic.

Recognize that real estate is a game of numbers.

The entire thing boils down to percentages. You're going to need to look at a lot of property and make a bunch of deals. At the time you can make the offer, you could be looking at as many as a hundred or so properties. And instead, after studying the homes and looking at the pictures, you might be able to limit the initial hundred down to maybe 25 that you're highly interested in, so maybe you'll make your bid on just 10 of them. You're going to need the passion to help you through this process. You should remain realistic and realize that only one house in ten turns into a purchase. What you can do is make deals that you know will work for you from a numerical point of view, and then let the chips fall when they do. You can't get close to any property, and you don't know which one you're really going to end up with. To look at properties, be available always. You're going to need to be accommodating and ready to look at houses when they're open for viewing, even though it's not easy for you. You'll need to be alert to look at the houses on Sunday mornings or Tuesday evenings, or anytime the property is open for viewing.

Understand why you never know which house you're going to get in advance.

A lot of times, when you put an offer on the house, you just don't know which one you're going to get. You might end up with the house you figured was least likely to go your way. You never learn why. When it's a bank-owned building, you're not going to know the bank's situation and what their needs are. It's the same thing with the selling of the house. The best thing is not to care about the asking price and not to think over how the bid should be approved.

Your market plan will decide the bid, not the asking price.

Don't think about the list price, because the list price just doesn't have anything to do with what the business plan is. If your business strategy is to position a bid at a certain proportion of what you believe the after-repaired benefit is, you can position the bid irrespective of the selling price. You never know what the vendor is going to consider, and you don't know what the bank has in it. The bank may have bought a note back for pennies on the dollar, and now they're just scrambling to get what they've got out of the building. But don't be afraid to place a lot of offers in your houses.

Many of these points are very basic, but they are also important to understand and follow. Be reminded of the few nuts and bolts of the real estate business:

· Remain calm but don't ever get sentimental about the house.

· It's a game of numbers, and the more offers you put in, the better your chances.

· You 're just on holiday. Be available to look at assets at any moment.

· You can't tell which house is going to come through for you, and it isn't going to.

· Don't care about the price of the list. Make a deal that is in accordance with your schedule.

You just don't know when the deal is going to go through, so if you obey these basic rules, you'll be in perfect shape if and when the bid is approved.

BIGGEST HOME IMPROVING MISTAKES OF REAL ESTATE DEVELOPER

As a real estate developer, it is also a smart investment decision to make home renovations on whatever real estate you buy. There are a variety of common mistakes surrounding home renovation and investment in real estate, and by understanding what such errors are, you can save a lot of time and make matters easier. Let the errors made by other real estate developers be your guide to what to avoid. The first error any real estate developers make is to purchase a home in a poor place or for more money than the house is worth. No matter how many home renovations you do on one of these houses, it's doubtful that you'll get a good income back, or even your money back.

Please weigh all of these considerations before you agree to invest in the property and upgrade it to your house. A grave error many real estate investors make is not knowing or finding out about the building codes in their area when they are making home improvements. Many developers don't get the required permits needed by the town where the property is located. That's one of the greatest mistakes, and if you do one, it will cost you a fortune. The construction inspector is there to ensure the changes to the house are safe and well completed. If a permit is necessary and you fail to obtain one, you will need to take down all work that has been completed, procure the permit and then continue from scratch.

A more frequent error committed by real estate developers is under budgeting for the home renovation scheme. The old saying was about taking the prices, then tripling them. That's an exaggeration, just by little. Many homeowners don't make a completely comprehensive budget down to the last nail and staple of what's required for the home improvement project. You would have a more balanced budget for being practical and budgeting for all available resources; you are far less likely to go over budget. You will also prepare for any possible eventuality that might arise and account for it in the budget to prevent any unnecessary and costly problems. The greatest single error committed by real estate developers is attempting to save money on home renovation by undertaking jobs themselves while they are not eligible. There are certain jobs a registered contractor or repairman may have on hand. A novice can easily take on certain home improvement projects and come out perfect, but professionals can only undertake other projects such as a new roof or some other comprehensive repairs. This is because these ventures entail multiple safety concerns, not just for the individual doing the job but also for any renters or owners who live in the building. Without making such mistakes, you will save a great deal of money on your real estate investment. Know the property's value before you purchase it, so you don't spend too much, and make sure the place is good. Make sure the estimate is practical, and it takes every possible piece of material and expense into account. Please make sure you are factoring in any potential unforeseen costs or issues. The biggest mistake to make is deciding when to ask for professional assistance and properly doing the home improvement project yourself.

HOW TO BUY PROPERTY FOR BACK TAXES AND LESS THAN $200 TO START

Even though you have very little capital to start with, it is now the time to break into the real estate investment market. In the past, there was never a time when so much opportunity for investors was present. Here's how to buy property for the return taxes-even if you have only $200-$500, to begin with. First, avoid buying property when tax is being sold. You could have worked this out already. If not, here's why you don't purchase properties for back taxes at tax sales: there's so much demand, so prices go so high; you can't check the properties until you purchase it; much of the time, the sellers pay off the debt, making you needless; so eventually, you've got to come up with your whole deal right there and then in cash. A much easier way to buy back-tax properties is directly from the sellers themselves-but only after-tax sales. By waiting until close to the end of the redemption cycle, you will not spend your time on properties with landowners who will pay the taxes back (they will have a mortgage by then), or properties with a mortgage (mortgage providers will have redeemed by then).

Everything that remains is people that can't pay and need to sell. Many buyers, having agreed to just let the property go, would have given up and carried on. These owners are your goose in cash. Offer to pay them to sign the deed to you ($200), so you can "see what you can do with it." Since the deed is worthless in their minds, a lot of people will just be happy to see $200 for you. Other owners still value their properties and know it is time to sell their properties. If / when you are finally willing to sell the land, give them $200 for their deed and plan to split the income. Or, bid them $200 and rent them back the house. Then, you just pay off the taxes, and it's your house. When you don't lend the house out to the lender, either you should sell or rent it. So if you have only the $200 to your credit, sell the property easily to another buyer by selling far below market value. You will still make a nice profit, and the new buyer will be able to tackle the tax problem. If you're looking to start investing for cheap, this is the only surefire way to get in on the tax sale property everyone is trying to get-and best of all when you're going after them; there's almost no competition for those properties.

PREPARING A STEP-BY-STEP REAL ESTATE REVIEW

Preparing an investment property analysis to determine if an investment is going to be good for you is paramount to successful real estate investment. Of note, a study of real estate is just as useful as the details you are gathering, and it provides no value to the investment targets when relevant statistics are used in the research.

PURCHASE PRICE

Okay, you've found a rental property that you like, but now you have to determine how the investment property looks financially as the broker tells you. The owner wants $500,000, saying he's practically "giving away" his home because the ten-unit building down the street sold for $530,000 last year, and his house is even more affordable as it has the lowest rentals in the city (suggesting you'll increase the rent and the gross income there). He likes his property in other words and supports his size. It is always up to you to determine whether the property is priced according to your own survey.

Present Loans

What guarantees are in place and should be taken for granted, and the lender should consider bringing a second mortgage.

Number of Units, Unit Mix

How many units the building has, and what the design or product combination is. How will occupant demand these setups line up?

Rental Income

How much annual the seller records rental income, and what vacancy rate? Any rental income that claims zero vacancies is not realistic and must include some vacancy allowance. Examine a current rent roll and pay careful attention to when the rates were last adjusted and whether they are fair according to your own rent report. Owners occasionally raise rents up to or beyond the market before selling the property, in turn passing on a bunch of disgruntled tenants who may move out soon. Search for an opportunity to increase rents, too.

Real Estate Tax

Ask the seller to show a current tax bill or contact the county tax collector's office to inquire about that information. For a fact, make an estimation of the property taxes you will be paying if you lease the rental house. For example, in California, property taxes are one percent of the sale price, which may be even higher than the purchaser paid.

Insurance scheme

Demand a copy of the insurance contract to make sure the coverage is appropriate for you; it may be old, which may well be far below the actual benefit of the changes. To be free, get a new tender.

Utilities & Trash

Ask the vendor to check whether he has paid for power, water and sewage, gas (if applicable), and waste disposal for the last two to three years (not in the last year).

Maintenance and Repairs

Just when the owner provides his estimates, measure your own repair and maintenance expenses because the owner may have done more or a part of his own repairs and maintenance, or maybe you would not have earned a discount. Six to eight percent of gross operating income is sufficient in most cases.

Grounds Care, Publicity, Pest Control

What has the developer charged to manage the property, probably to have a spa, and for advertising? Was there an additional cost to a pest management service? One of the most important questions you need to address is "about how do You want to get involved with your real estate investment operations?" Will you handle the property yourself, or in conjunction with an on-site manager, or will you hire a skilled contractor to operate the property for you?

PREPARE REVIEW

Well, you 're ready to get started with all those considerations in mind. A good investment software solution for real estate will be easy because it provides the forms, calculations, and reports.

1) Exhibit type of property (i.e., residential or commercial property), address, square footage, size, etc.

2) Present the total estimated revenue (i.e., the potential annual rental income as if the units were 100 percent).

3) Subtract a proportion of vacancy losses and incorporate total sales from other outlets such as coin-operated washers and dryers, storage facilities, etc. to measure gross operating income;

4) Subtract the total operating costs for measuring net taxable profit, such as property tax, insurance, electricity, etc. To determine the cap rate split this number by the sale price.

5) Deduct the gross interest balance before tax to determine the cash flow. Calculate the cash-on-cash return by dividing that by the overall contribution (i.e., down payment, purchase costs, and loan points).

6) Calculate the gross profit from net operating income by deducting the accumulated interest, amortized debt points, and depreciation allowance. To measure

your taxes owed (or tax savings) subtract that by the marginal income tax rate (i.e., state and federal taxes). If taxes are owed, subtract the amount from the pre-tax cash flow to measure the after-tax cash flow, and if taxes are avoided, then apply the amount to the pre-tax cash flow to determine the cash flow after tax. Know, this is made simple with a premium real estate investment tech solution.

The sequence with the correct data will tell you in a matter of minutes what you need to know about a particular property and will help you make a sound and knowledgeable investment decision.

HOW SUCCESSFUL INVESTORS PREPARE AN ANALYSIS OF THEIR REAL ESTATE

Productive real estate developers are never purely dependent on what some claim. When a prospective real estate purchase has been found, cautious owners conduct a tight analysis of the revenue, expenditures, cash flow, yield rates, and viability of the rental property. Regardless of what overzealous brokers or sellers say, watchful interest in real estate needs figures to be checked. To do this, real estate investors rely on a number of analyses and return expectations for calculating the financial success of an income property. And we'll find some of those records and financial indicators in this post.

REPORTS

Perhaps the annual property operational results, or APOD, are the most common reports used in real estate investment circles. It is because, within the first year of possession, an APOD offers the real estate analyst a simple appraisal or "snapshot" of property results. It does not consider tax shelter, but it can serve as the immovable equivalent of an annual income and expense statement by a properly created APOD. A Declaration of Proforma Income is also common among analysts. Although containing estimated figures, a proforma provides a convenient means for real estate investors and analysts to determine the potential, long-term cash flow, success of an investment property. For a span of 10 to 20 years, Proformas periodically forecasts numbers out. The Rent Roll is certainly one of the most relevant records for an examination of the real estate. This is because the sources of income and revenue stream of a property are vital to making wise investment decisions about real estate. A rent roll usually includes buildings already leased with existing leases, along with empty units and rentals on the market. Rents displayed in the rent roll will, of course, be checked by the tenants through due diligence.

RETURN TICKETS

Some of the most common rates of return used by real estate investors are the rate of capitalization or cap rate. That is because the cap rate gives a simple first glance view of the willingness of a property to pay its own way by communicating the balance between the valuation of a property and its net operating profit. Cap rate also offers a convenient way for real estate buyers to evaluate comparable assets.

Cash-on - cash return compares the ratio of the projected first-year cash flow of a property to the amount of money used to buy the land. While cash on capital return does not compensate for the time value of assets or cash flows beyond the first year, this limitation is often ignored because it offers a convenient means for property owners to easily compare the viability of comparable income-producing properties and investment opportunities.

The internal rate of return is more complicated because it needs a time-value measurement of capital and thus needs a financial calculator or decent software for investment in real estate. Nevertheless, it is commonly used by economists as the intrinsic rate of return shows in quantitative terms what the original capital expenditure of an immovable lender would deliver on the basis of the estimated supply of potential cash flows adjusted to match the dollars currently. In other words, the intrinsic return factor transforms tomorrow's dollars into today's dollars and then determines the investment return.

Taking the time to do an in-depth real estate study. Create documents or returns and keep the figures light. That is the only fairly secure way to make the correct investment judgment on any prospective investment in real estate. Whether you do your property research correctly, you'll know whether the purchase makes good financial sense or not, so you'll almost definitely guarantee success in investing your real estate.

YOUR REAL ESTATE INVESTMENT MODEL

You can do some things before you launch this venture when you decide to get involved in real estate investment. You would want to make sure you make a sound investment decision, and learning the real estate terms and concepts is only one way to know how to make a good investment. However, perhaps most important of all is understanding the investment concept of immovable financial properties. It is an overview that will help you decide what funding opportunities you may have and help you build an operating strategy for your investment in real estate. A good investment model in financial, real estate will help ensure this endeavor is a profitable one. Until you can measure your investment plan in financial, real estate, you first need to do property analysis. You'll want to review all of the property's documents. The past of renting is really relevant to decide whether this would be a good venture for you. The expense of utility rates, premiums and benefits, fees, loan records, and previous loan payment background are all relevant to help you make this investment decision. All this information should be gathered accordingly from a study.

Analysis of these items is crucial to your investment model for real estate. For example, if you conclude that the property in the past has had a poor rental history or has not increased the value for many years, you may find the property to be a high-risk real estate. However, there are a couple of other factors to consider in helping you determine this. This is important if another detail is used in the real estate investment plan. Information on all the determinants of the cash flow is just as critical as the others. You may want to be sure you have information on all of the property's maintenance expenses, including any that can be collected by the owners and others that can't, construction expenses, vacancy rates, etc. non-occupancy damages including any other property-related costs. A financial investment model would be generated from all the information collected on the property, including information such as business history, environment, and any possible developments that could impact the property's value.

The data will be inputted into your real estate investment model when you have all the appropriate details. Some developers prefer to use software applications specially designed by real estate buyers, while others use Excel to evaluate the data they've collected. You can find many of the tech programs online or at the big software firms. Once you have inputted the information, the analysis will start, and you will be able to determine whether or not the property you are considering will be a good investment. Without a successful investing plan for real estate to go into, you take the opportunity to purchase high-risk assets that may result in a capital loss rather than a capital gain. To help you decide whether a property is a suitable investment or not, study the investing model you would use carefully by telling people what they are using and talking to real estate brokers specializing in investment properties.

SIX ECONOMIC CRITERIA ON REAL ESTATE VALUATION

Real estate valuation determines a specific price that one will pay to buy a particular property in practical terms. Naturally, the most common approach for residential property valuation to brokers and agents is the comparative market analysis (or CMA). The land appraisal method entails calculating the value of certain equivalent (or comparable) properties in the same business region or certain related markets depending on the sale values. Usually, when planning a CMA, it is used to assume the price of the relevant property, a total of three comparable properties recently sold, and three comparable properties actually for sale. The discrepancies between the equivalent properties and the subject property are measured in order to increase or reduce the interest in the comparison and measure the fair market value of the subject property using a comparative method. Various economic principles largely influence commercial property assessment (i.e., office buildings, apartment buildings, single-family communities, and land plots). Usually, these values are not factored into the standard residential property CMA survey. This book aims to shed some light on these values since they can be extended to any attempt to evaluate land. They are the basis for our emphasis in this discussion, as we look at and outline six applicable economic concepts that can help give you an understanding of the effect they can have on a property's valuation.

1) Anticipation

This is supposed to offer additional benefits. In other words, real estate owners are calculating the value of real estate assets on the basis of the property's expected potential revenue stream. Instead of the perceived market value inferred by a comparative analysis, or the construction and land costs required to replace the property, they are more likely to value a property on the revenue it generates. The assets planned, or predicted, capability for producing profit is the primary objective. For someone with an awareness of commercial real estate acquisition, this strategy is not a surprise; however, the ordinary property owner or investor may not have a common experience. The emphasis on buying expected cash flows will also extend the perception of residential properties' valuation. Instead of thinking, for example, "how much is worth the property now," think, "how much return would you buy the property and rent it later." This method and experience will make all the difference in a competitive climate.

2) Compliance

This is characterized as the need at a given location for fair similarity and compatibility. For instance, compatible land uses may produce higher values than those with location-imposed limits on the property. For example, the most likely value of an apartment complex located in a primarily residential area is more than one located in a highly industrial zone. Savvy commercial real estate developers are keen on this idea, although other homeowners may not pay much attention to surrounding or neighboring land uses. From an investment viewpoint, taking a wider view of the relevant uses will provide a better interpretation of value or potential value.

3) Supply & Demand

This principle concerns both the shortage and the subject property market. Although investment real estate with similar physical and economic characteristics can sell at similar values, real estate value can be significantly influenced (higher or lower) within a market that lacks a fair equilibrium between supply and order. For instance, land in a metropolitan region where undeveloped land is scarce will need more valuation than land in a rural area with large vacant land parcels. Similarly, an apartment building that sells at a time where there is more than enough capacity to satisfy the rental demand will have less benefit for a real estate buyer than the same building at a time where the availability of apartments in the city is smaller and is not fulfilling the demand adequately.

4) Best and Highest Use

This is an important principle that applies to optimum use and best possible use of a resource, as opposed to its actual use. When it is technically necessary to change the use of a sufficiently compliant, physically feasible, and commercially sustainable property, the value of the same property will be substantially improved. For instance, an office building can be enlarged to include more cost-effective office space or first-floor retail; or an apartment complex can add additional units or incorporate mixed-use options to maximize the neighborhood's appeal. Investors and developers in commercial real estate use this principle to create value and increase the cash flow. The concept can also be applied in suburban real estate where a developer or owner of a residential property assesses the land's greatest and optimal use under the urban zoning and building codes and proposes enhancing or increasing the attributes and characteristics of the property to maximize their worth.

5) Contribution

This essentially means that if it is physically, legally, and economically feasible to contribute more space to the property at a cost equal to, or less than, the marginal revenue it generates, the value of income property can be impacted. In other words, the risk of making the commitment or the transaction is offset as value-added. Unlike the principle of highest and best use, this principle compares revenue or value with the benefits that may be produced by the investment or contribution. The question to ask after you have identified the highest and best use of your property is whether or is justifiable, the investment or contribution required to achieve the highest and best use for the property makes financial sense. You can attach amenities to a home such as a pool and a patio, and you can attach units to a multi-family building; the issue of commitment is, "will you be willing to sell the house for the additional profit you know you are making, or will you rent the new apartment units?"

6) Substitution

This is a term on the cost of opportunity. In other words, a rational real estate investor will not pay for an investment property than how it will yield in financial benefit what the next best substitute with similar levels of risk will. This means examining all other options well for residential buyers, owners, or investors. Residential home buyers often fall in love with the home they see first or second, and as a result, can easily forget about better opportunities. This principle suggests the assessment and comparison of numerous market opportunities before making a decision. The six principles listed in this article are intended as an outline to give you an idea of how other economic factors can influence property valuation. Though these principles are demonstrated in the valuation of commercial real estate, they also affect residential properties and should be observed when analyzing the value of any real estate.

3 ROOKIE REAL ESTATE ANALYSIS MISTAKES TO AVOID

An immovable property appraisal is a standard for creditors and analysts seeking to assess the cash flows, return expectations, and productivity efficiency of any future investment opportunity. It is a straightforward operation. Financial information of the rental property is collected (i.e., net revenue, operating costs, and mortgages), and the figures are mathematically "crunched" to calculate the bottom line cash flow, return values, and productivity that the owner would expect to gain by owning the estate. Consequently, the need to construct a sound real estate report with reasonable figures is a must for the developer to make the appraisal and, eventually, real estate investment decisions. Nevertheless, it is common for less seasoned agents and inexperienced buyers to unwittingly distort the bottom line with incorrect data due to their lack of expertise in analyzing the data correctly.

1. Vacancy factor

The income stream that an investment property produces is of paramount importance to an investor because that's what determines the bottom line. However, rental revenue must also be offset by the number of empty units that the property has. For example, a ten-unit apartment building could generate a monthly income of $10,000 if all ten units are rented out for $1,000 a month. If two of those units are unoccupied, on the other hand, the actual monthly income would be only $8,000. Okay, but here's where novices have a propensity to fail. The vacancy rate factor actually faced by the company is regularly seen-often, even at zero percent. But with a new owner, maybe this isn't the truth. Bear in mind that business pressures, wear and tear on land, rent changes and even a change of ownership will (and sometimes does) cause vacancies. And as you build a real estate report, look at the past and current financial results of a company, and do have a vacancy reserve characteristic of the local market. If there's a need to believe otherwise, a 5 percent figure is normally suitable for vacancies and mostly used by bank appraisers.

2. Maintenance and restorations

The cost of managing and replacing a profit property is an ongoing burden that must be paid by each owner when appliance pieces split, and screens tear. However, constructing an estimate based on the total cost that the current owner spends on maintenance upgrades during his ownership is an error, as it might not be applicable to what a potential owner may spend in the future. For e.g., the current owner may have benefited from reduced prices if he or she did their own maintenance, or perhaps had a close relative who did. On the other side, the new owner would be forced to contract all of the high dollar repairs and upkeep out. This is important not to ignore what the landlord spent to manage the rental house but make sure also to include a proportion of the gross operating profit that best represents what a potential owner would have to pay for.

3. Substitute Funds

Replacement reserves are money that a real estate investor sets aside to cover any future replacements for worn-out items that he or she may incur upon purchase of the property. It is not an ongoing cost that the owner will periodically pay in order to maintain the property in operation, such as income taxes, electricity, or garbage. It's smart to find an alternative capital allocation upfront so the borrower can have a more specific look at the company's expected cash flows and return values. Many observers annually expect this based on x-dollars per server. For example, if the property consists of twenty units and the analyst wants to use a $300 per unit value, then the property valuation will represent the $6,000 annual amount.

THE BENEFIT OF REAL ESTATE ANALYSIS SOFTWARE

Crunching rental property cash flows, rates of return, and profitability numbers adequately enough for investors to make prudent real estate investment decisions can be quite labor-intensive. In fact, it's very time consuming before the invention of computing technologies, as it allowed the researcher to calculate and manually print the data manually. Today, however, with the advent of third-party tech tools, relying on apps has become standard practice for consumers and analysts to do the number crunching for them. Nevertheless, not everybody who deals with rental income properties and does an overview of the real estate knows this benefit. Strangely enough, in this era of automation, it's not unusual to find investors and agents who often manually calculate and print the data. Therefore, it's important to address the issue and make a statement for the advantages of using apps to all of you who remain uncommitted. Nonetheless, rest assured that one's intention is not to highlight any single software feature, but rather to get you to think about the "technology" as a whole. In other words, ideally, as you know how we performed an "old days" real estate study, you can come to understand more thoroughly why tech has advanced, the challenges it addresses, and how you can make a profit at the end.

ORIGIN

The challenge of generating a cash balance and measurement of the cost of return has been around as long as real estate investment. Indeed, it is hard to believe that any developer has not used any tool in history to evaluate whether a property will result in a benefit or not. Of reality, before the invention of computers, the method had to be performed manually at all times. For example, only as recently as the early 1990s, you can perform an overview of real estate with a calculator in one hand, and pencil and paper in the other. Many of you remember the struggles and difficulties those of us working with income property had to resolve manually in those "early days."

THE FACTS

The data associated with investment real estate is the heart and soul of any real estate analysis. Of reality, it goes without thinking. To assess its particular value, the real estate investor needs to consider the property's financial performance. Before computer programs, however, this presented several problems. Foremost, particularly for novices, it was not always known what data was needed for a realistic bottom-line. For e.g., what constitutes the operating expenses of a rental property? Or what details are required to get the net operating profit, cash flow, or rate of return of property? What needs to be included to make projections for revenue? And so, it was. Since the correct data is provided at the same time, an accurate calculation of the numbers is crucial. As a result, the laborious task of checking and rechecking numbers was always there to ensure accuracy. Before computers and automated systems by third parties came along the process.

THE FORMULAS

A variety of returns on real estate owners focus on calculating the valuation of an income-producing property to allow the buyer to assess whether they compete with their particular investment targets or whether their interest stakes up against the prices of comparable types of property in the surrounding business region. As a result, creditors are looking at returns such as cap cost, gross rent multiplier, cash-on-cash, internal rate of return, among many others. Many of these returns require basic arithmetic that can be calculated almost in one's brain. But other returns are, therefore, much more nuanced. Return values correlated with tax shelter components, and the time-value of capital, for example, would definitely require nothing less than a financial calculator. The argument is that each return represents a formula, and such formulas had to be mastered before technical solutions. A computer or third-party software program can't guarantee a successful investment in your real estate. Whether you own the most sophisticated Mac, the most recent MS Excel edition, or maybe even more than one tech tool for real estate analysis, you're not off the hook. You always have to do your homework and research. But, if you want to use it, there is a value to this technology.

ANALYZE YOUR PROSPECTIVE INVESTMENT IN REAL ESTATE FROM TOP TO BOTTOM

If you're a conservative real estate investor, and we'll assume you 're, you need to carefully and thoroughly analyze it once you're locating your prospective real estate investment. You need to check all the information about the house, especially the seller's income and expenses. You never have to count on exactly what you think. Create an inventory of the property that contains documentation such as an APOD, Proforma Income Statement, and Rent Roll. Such types of real estate review report often act as a checklist for things you want to know, such as a number of units, age of the house, rent breakdown per unit, cost items, lot size, land and place features, and so on, while helping you make a wise investment decision. You will find a tool to assist you with real estate investing tools. When the rental property does not appear to be financially valuable after the initial appraisal has been made, maybe adjusting one or more of these will change the financial picture and make the property a good investment in real estate. Analyze future real estate investment using the list of the separate processes below.

1) Income: Can rents be increased, and can they be increased soon after you purchase the property? Would a shift in the form of the occupant in the building permit higher rentals, possibly due to bad or non-existent management suffer in some cases? Can the building be used to collect revenue, such as a hotel or small offices, or other ways? Being aware of the current code makes any improvements proposed. Is it fair to believe that the property might have certain revenue, such as a co-operated laundry service, garages, or storage rooms?

2) Costs: Review running costs carefully to see if any of them was unnecessary. If there is, is it reasonable to think you can lower them down? Of course, you can't manage any cost, but if you plan to do your own lawn care and renovations, you can save some money.

3) Funding: Asset returns can be modified easily by applying various financing strategies. While one form of financing plan could make your prospective real estate investment look unprofitable, another funding method could make your prospective property a safe, productive investment as quickly as possible. Test various funding options to see how the mortgage impacts cash balance, yield rates, and productivity.

4) Money flow: Don't just consider the before-tax cash flow produced by the investment real estate to determine your overall benefits. Look at the after-tax cash flow to figure out what your property can give you in the after-tax return form. Consideration of tax avoidance components such as paper loss that the IRS

provides for redemption (cost recovery) is also preferred. Also, good tools for real estate investing will render the calculation in seconds for you, so it doesn't have to be complicated.

5) Price: Many rental properties would actually not make sense, regardless of other considerations, unless the landlord is willing to negotiate a lower price. To increase your chances for success, however, don't simply throw out a number. If a seller gets the impression that your numbers have no rationale, they'll be less willing to discuss a price with you. Tweak the price beforehand to see if there are any effects on the cash flow and return rates. Then, pick a price based on the rates of return most attractive. Prepare and address those estimates with the seller. You may be shocked to see a salesman able to listen to reason. The argument in these statistics has to make sense. Never make a decision to purchase investment properties based on the building's esthetic attractiveness or use a basic thumb rule to assess its worth. Note, even women are attractive, and the numbers are all about real estate investment. Take the time to do an overview of the land. This is the most fairly secure way to make the correct investment judgment on any prospective investment in real estate. If your property analysis shows that the property doesn't make financial sense, forget how pretty it may be and don't buy it!

HOME PRICE-HOW TO NEGOTIATE LIKE A PRO

Home buying can be an exciting thing to do. This is because a great deal of deep understanding is needed for the whole process of home acquisition. In order to get into the buying process, you have to learn how to negotiate. Of course, you do not immediately give in to the initial offer of the broker. As much as possible, you want to haggle it until you arrive at your desired price. If you are totally unaware of how to deal with the seller, don't worry, there is an easy way of learning the process. Perhaps you'd like to look at these methods and specifics of how to compromise like a pro.

COMPARABLE STUDY OF THE MARKETS

When you've already seen the house you want, calculating the fair value is the initial step in the negotiation. This method indicates what similar properties were sold for at the site. You can get the details about the Comparable study of the markets from the real estate broker. There are real estate websites that can display free estimators of the property value that will allow you to test the sale prices of houses in your future neighborhood. This method normally helps you to decide whether the bid is a fair price for you. The values of the sold property can be seen. You will then compare the prices listed against the bid issued since these figures are usually not the best measures of what the property will sell for. Between the two quantities, there will be a significant difference. Generally, the Comparable study of the markets provides you with specific information on the homes being compared: number of bedrooms and relaxation rooms, square feet, price list, and price of sale. Only concentrate on the related property you want, take a look at their definition and location. And ensuring the data is revised to prevent any number miscalculations.

STATUS OF THE PROPERTY

The value or state has a significant effect on the property 's overall sale price. This will lead to the question if the house you want is outstanding from the rest of the properties sold? Create a reasonable assessment of the situation, and analyze it all.

EXTRA FACILITIES

You definitely want to live in a house that has a full set of high-class amenities, right? Also, if there is just a slight effect on the valuation of additional services, without the location and situation, but it may also be a consideration. Be careful because you might be too engrossed with the high-tech kitchen facilities in the house that you like, but it will not have a major impact on the property's value if you resell it.

ENTHUSIASM

Great negotiators collate as much information about the land and the buyers as possible. The proprietor 's intent for which the property is being sold must be at its top. Is it really necessary to sell the house? If the broker who speaks for you is a buyer's agent, they will seek to give you the detail. But if you are dealing with a broker that speaks for the seller, they normally keep this info not until the seller tells them to share it.

PREPARING

You have to always be careful, as you strive to be a strong negotiator. Your attitude is the prime factor. Don't let your common sense consume feelings as you bargain. Set a fair cap and be strict in that regard. When you don't agree with the price, then simply drop it.

PROVIDING DEALS AND NEGOTIATION STRATEGIES FOR BUYERS IN REAL ESTATE

To the Real Estate Investor who has purchased or sold an excellent investment opportunity, nothing can bring more joy than realizing that you have done a fine job negotiating the price and terms of the contract. While there will be occasions where a great chance may be "given" or "giving-away" depending on drastic motivating reasons such as divorce, foreclosures, disability, etc. Many agreements would require an amount of sharing from both sides and will take effort. While all discussions will have a win/win plan and end target, it is typically the side who has planned the most effective that will come away with a bigger slice of the pie from the table. The guide was written to provide an outline of the basic negotiating strategies you may like to add. The following text is broken down into sections beginning with some background information and leading up into the three stages negotiating cycles.

PRACTICING NEGOTIATIONS BY ROLE PLAYING

All successful negotiators have laid out their own approach style of negotiating. It would be important for you to focus on your strategy whilst practicing as a negotiator and change it when you see how things turn out. One common form of training that can help you develop more confidence in your discussions is to play a part. Playing a role will allow you to experiment with your approach and build more confidence without fear of losing a deal. If possible, carry out the role-playing session with someone who has negotiating experience so they can provide constructive feedback on the session. One strategy that can give you valuable feedback when you perform your role-playing sessions is to film them or do a video recording, much better. Having the opportunity to revisit those sessions would be highly helpful in your negotiating skills growth. You will "see" the change you are making over time, from getting videos.

REASONS FOR REJECTION

There are several reasons why you do not accept the proposals, or you can't even get them to decide to meet you. You can come across several people who are in tough, even life-threatening circumstances during your real estate investing journey. The successful negotiator will attempt to embrace possible grounds for refusal and adjust their approach with that person based on the particular situation. The following segment will outline the most common explanations for rejection and will include guidance for how to overcome their pushback by altering the approach.

EXPLAIN WHY THIS CONTRACT IS PERFECT FOR THE OTHER SIDE

As part of your negotiation plan, you can have a dialogue about whether they can profit from the deal you are making. In certain cases, their possible advantages may be very familiar and intuitive to the other side. And, while that is not going to be the case, you will come across possibilities. Let's say, as an example, you 're trying to convince a property owner to keep a mortgage, and they're inexperienced in that field. If you give an overview of the anticipated principal and interest payments verses that they take a lump sum at closing, you may be able to convince them that this option might be better than relying on typical investment instruments such as CDs, mutual funds, etc.

"EDUCATE"

You may need to give some information to the people on the other side of the table as part of your negotiation plan. Throwing out an unsuccessfully orchestrated bid that is a ludicrous bid in other parties' eyes would just make them fight back even more or maybe dismiss the contract. However, if you know that the other side's stance might be founded on incorrect data, then you can take advantage of the chance and provide some evidence that may allow them to see things correctly. You may have a clear profit in their eyes, of course, so they believe they have to disregard your results. However, to give it a try will definitely be worth your time. An example of that might be to suggest that they have a Pro forma showing a potential vacancy rate and you know that is understated, maybe if you were to collect statistics from the nearby property management firm detailing the real vacancy rates incomparable properties, you would be in a position to discuss more. One way to establish credibility in this situation is to disclose the source of your data and suggest that you use a third party to confirm the information you provided to them.

FIND A CONNECTION WITH THE OTHER SIDE

Breaking the ice on a new relationship or negotiation can truly be beneficial by discussing non-business and non-confrontational topics. Through this strategy, you will ease the conversation of doing business gently. Furthermore, these group conversations will provide you with some hints as to who you are working with and whether you need actually to alter your strategy. Certain examples of ice breaker formation based on your initial observations may include:

O Seen Family Photos

O Amazing home décor

O Showed Art and Trophies

O Pick up the car on the driveway

O A knowledge of each other

MAKING THE PACKAGE

Based on the sort of talks that you are trying to participate in, you might want to add some punch to your bid by designing a beautiful looking kit that you will hand away at the conference. The kit will contain different bits of details to help you close the bid, and the following highlights can be included:

O A snapshot into the past

O An outline of the business

O Your Offer highlights

O Historical information to better back the bid

O The other hand must know the anticipated benefits

The use of maps, diagrams, and photographs can make the analysis more meaningful and compelling. The only issue with this strategy is that if you hand out the kit, having all players on the same page (literally) might be difficult; it would be a common inclination for them to search the document while you're talking.

CREATE A VISUAL PRINT

Another choice is to use a digital display when delivering the offer; this choice would help you to monitor the details that the party is viewing and at what time during the negotiations. This "looking forward" will discourage them. Once you've finished your presentation, you should still present them with a hard copy.

KNOW YOUR RESTRICTIONS

This would be incredibly necessary for you to pre-determine the contract's parameters when you build your negotiation strategy. You should have limits on the substantial aspects of the deal. Unless such thresholds are reached, a red flag may be raised that you will have to compromise and walk away. Those restrictions can include:

O Sales price

o Closing date

O Mortgage terms

o Repair credits

If you can have to make certain compromises or decisions on the fly during the talks, without getting such pre-determined boundaries, during the excitement of the negotiating process, you may become very fragile.

Given the ideal potential partnership with the other hand, the degree of commitment in keeping the ground on the bid and terms may be altered. If you're trying to develop a long-term friendship with them, you might be more open to giving up more. If you know that this is a one-shot deal with these guys, it could mean you're going to hold to your guns and make no more concessions.

SUBMIT A SEALED BID

Depending on the case, all of the negotiating strategies listed in this document do not work when presenting a sealed bid, as you might not be given a chance to negotiate at all. This condition can be identified where the responsibility for liquidating real and personal properties has been transferred to a third party involved. A foreclosure or land selling is one example of this. By the day, the sealed bids are released. Usually, the highest offer made will be in a position to purchase the house. When you face this challenge, the only choice is to apply the best deal that also makes sense for the company.

DON'T GO IN WITH YOUR BEST SHOT

When you build your negotiation approach, keeping off from sharing the best bid just outside the gate would be crucial. When you start off with something less than the best possible bid, that will allow you the space to compromise against the role of the other side. Consider what's going to run through their heads if you actually come out and said, "This is the most I can do, and it's not negotiable." Maybe they'd either give in and consider the bid or know you're not interested in "letting the relationship grow" and talked them off on another contract.

ASK FOR THINGS YOU DON'T EVEN NEED

A common negotiation strategy is to press for items or concessions that are not necessarily required or desirable with the political goal of delivering them to the other side as a means to show the intention to "win the deal" An example of this strategy is selling a house and having a closing date of 30 days even though you are completely comfortable with a closing date of 60 to 90 days. Through encouraging the customer to have "free time," another party will have the power to change their stance on certain conditions that are more important for you.

USING TIMELINES FOR YOUR ADVANTAGE

As a way to add additional leverage to your offer and approach to negotiation, you should try to understand if any critical deadlines are approaching that might help your position. For example, if you know that a seller has a balloon payment due in 30 days ' time, it can be expected that they will usually get more driven as the date passes. So, seek to arrange the meetings at best possible time where possible.

PERFORMING YOUR DUE DILIGENCE

As you plan for the negotiating session and develop your approach, you can take this time to conduct as much due diligence as you can. Such due investigation will help reinforce your role as well as help verify any evidence from the other side that is given to you.

LEARN HOW TO PREDICT

A good negotiator will also spend time in thinking about the offer they are seeking to "secure" from the other people's mindsets. When you construct your contract, you need to recognize all of the challenges and problems that will be presented theoretically and come up with a solution to those issues before the meeting. Another approach that can help you recognize those problems is to assume that on the other hand, you are negotiating this contract. With this strategy, you can eliminate the risk of hitting broadside with a question that you have not thought. Nothing instills confidence in the person you are communicating than offering rational answers to all potential problems and scenarios.

HAVING A SCRIPT

This may be useful for you to have a memorized template that you can use in your negotiating sessions based on the type of discussions you usually deal with. Using a "canned" strategy can aid when operating with a similar business model repeatedly, which can help ensure continuity, which is maintained from session to session. This version should evolve over time and will be updated based on the lessons learned from previous sessions of negotiations.

LETTER OF UNDERSTANDING

You will need to create a paper, called the Letter of Intent (LOI), at some stage during the production of the offer and the negotiating phase. The registered contract is not the loi. These can also define the terms and conditions to be offered. The LOI can also serve as a basis for the creation of a Sales Agreement or Contract. The LOI can be the only way to deliver the agreement where face-to-face or telephone meetings are not acceptable or permissible.

PRESENT ONLY ONE CHOICE

You may want to consider offering several options or deals that are similarly advantageous to you in order to increase the chances for the deal to fly. This scenario would allow the other side to observe the versatility and set the stage for closing off further deals.

SECURE THE CONTRACT

There will be occasions where the topics or information that may be discussed during an offering and negotiations are confidential and should not be disclosed to anyone outside of the deal. That sort of scenario is very normal on larger deals, which may trigger any problems if the details are revealed to the general public. Another definition of that might be an investor who owns a shopping center and who doesn't want to meet the tenants. Usually, a Non-Disclosure Agreement (NDA) is executed when such a situation is necessary. The NDA is a legally binding agreement that would signify that it does not disclose the specifics of this contract or bid with anyone in the transaction. In fact, when you collect this sensitive material, it will write out the intensions. When any material is improperly exchanged, it may lead to a court case.

YOUR APPEARANCE

When planning for the negotiating conference, it's important to look appropriate, depending on who your conference and what the situation is. If you meet for dinner, for example, with very successful businessmen, you want to dress to impress, which would have formal business wear. In comparison to that, you do not want to look so fancy if you see a homeowner who is about to lose their house. Based on their implicit assumptions that you are doing very well financially, and why would they offer away more, walking in with your custom-designed suit will affect this discussion. In fact, under-dressing may even send inappropriate signals in this case.

NEGOTIATE HERE WITH EVERYONE

When presenting or negotiating an offer, you should always make sure all parties responsible for making a decision are present. Nothing can undermine your well-planned by negotiating more than critical people not present. Unless you rely entirely on the person you met to relay your bid's specifics, you may find yourself at a disadvantage. There may be situations that may prohibit you from getting there, but it's the desirable goal that you should aspire to accomplish.

ALWAYS NEGOTIATE, AND PRESENT OFFERS TO DECISION-MAKERS DIRECTLY WHEN POSSIBLE

You may come across situations where you negotiate and present offers to someone officially working on behalf of decision-makers. This relationship is very common with traditional contracts listing Seller / Broker. Usually, a buyer will present their offer in writing, and it may go through one or more real estate professionals before it ultimately comes to consideration by the seller. When the purchaser does not approve the bid and probably makes a counter-offer, it would have to appeal to the buyer through the same contact chain. While this situation can be tolerated on a "straight and clean" deal, when creative offers are presented that require a higher level of dialogue, it could be an extreme disadvantage.

THE SETTING OF THE NEGOTIATIONS

All of the planning time and well-planned negotiation tactics can not achieve the desired outcomes if you are not given the necessary time to address and resolve the agreement in the proper environment properly. While arranging discussions with the other parties, you need to be informed that this is important to your negotiation success. When scheduling a meeting, the following should illustrate circumstances you can avoid:

O Place for loud conference

O The Restaurants

O Lounges for Cocktails

O Workplaces

O Keeping little people diverted from the debate

O Meeting them when you know a team has less time limit than what you need.

MANY METHODS FOR CONTACT

Negotiate by phone

If telephone talks cannot be stopped, it is recommended that all relevant information which may be useful would be shared with all important parties at the time of the talks. Such details do not contain data that could weaken the bargaining position. Several things to remember about using communication techniques:

O Have the time slot pre-arranged when everyone's open.

O You might not know that anyone else will listen in to the conversation. It's recommended you inquire to see who's there.

O They could be recording the discussion

O Discourage mobile phone communications due to the risk of dropped calls and bad connections.

WEBINAR:

A webinar incorporates the phone's use to communicate directly by using a screen to view the information being addressed. Another approach that you may like to suggest is getting a webinar to present your offer. There are available programs that can have those capabilities.

Try to Be in Their Face

This is a major help if you are lucky enough to present an offer or bargain with the decision-makers directly. To take advantage of this to the highest point, it is highly advised that you do your negotiations face to face. Other forms of delivering the bid can not be used on an extraordinary basis, whether by telephone or by fax. There could be a condition that prohibits you from going face to face with them. A case in point would be an out-of-town owner or investor.

Walking Out of Contract

Despite all feudal bargaining efforts on both sides, there may be times when you just have to walk away from the deal because critical issues and terms could not be resolved. It is necessary to end the talks on good terms and with respect. If both sides do so, at a certain point in time, that might set the tone for joint partnership cooperation or even a reversal of the initial contract.

After you've decided this offer isn't right for you, it may be a perfect time to suggest that you have other investor associates involved in this idea. It could turn a wasted initiative otherwise into a possible referral fee or aid in forming a new partnership.

What Most people don't keep in mind during the negotiations

They don't recognize or reveal any signs of vulnerability. Beware of any tips that your body language may give away. This would be a perfect chance for the seasoned leader on the other side to take advantage of those limitations.

Don't mock someone by making them look dumb, or try to make them more persuasive. Such tactics would just place the other side on the defensive, and maybe widen the distance between the sides. Please be a professional, and be polite.

Don't talk about your past wins; it's cool to use previous success stories to prove you can make deals, but be careful how you're framing them.

Don't be so nervous about selling your position that you're doing all the talk. Be a better listener. By doing so, you'll be able to absorb the point of view of the other side.

O Don't think every moment should be packed with the conversation. Allow time to sink in on your comments. Remember this saying, "Silence can be deafening!"

HOW TO PLAY A STALE MATE

You can find that you can't come to any conclusion on a certain point during the talks. If this occurs, it is suggested that you park this issue momentarily and go on to other facets of the talks and then return to this issue later; maybe one of the parties can step away from their former stance and break the impasse.

ADJUST THE FLY THEME

When the talks begin, identifying the personalities you are working with and changing the conference's mood accordingly would be critical. For example, you may consider that the other party is a serious, stone-faced diplomat who does not understand your attitude to laughter.

BRING IN YOUR TEAM

While most typical one-on-one negotiations are done, there might be occasions where it would be helpful for you to call in other members of your team to engage in different areas of the negotiations. An example of this could be if you are evaluating financial data; during this negotiation area, you may want your accountant to be involved. Besides knowing the other side's strengths and weaknesses, it'll be critical for you to know your team's same information. You never want to put yourself in a position in which you don't know if your staff can manage the talks or what the vulnerabilities are. So, reiterate a prior argument, role-playing may also be successful in helping to build an overarching approach for team negotiation.

Don't Take Turns

If the talks have been concluded and you have a meeting of minds from both sides, stop re-starting the discussions by posing very small concerns and expect more compromises. Although there might be occasions where re-negotiations are needed (like when the due diligence uncovered high substantial maintenance costs). Don't let the smallest things get in the way of this deal happening. The last thing you expect is to get angry with you on the other hand and maybe even step back on their previous approval of the deal. When you decide to hammer out the deals, it's called Re-trading because someone else feels they 're done. Re-trading may create confusion on the other side and likely on certain Brokers involved. Stop trying to get every buck out of a contract; it could potentially damage any potential business partnerships you are seeking to build.

WHAT TO DO WHEN NEGOTIATIONS ARE OVER

LEARNT LESSONS

This would be very useful to remember what works and what does not work for your strategy when improving your negotiating skills, and to create a checklist on all the things you have learned. While it is possible that you can learn more about the stuff that went wrong in certain cases than the things that went right, you continue to take all of these experiences to fine-tune the strategies in preparation for the next task in negotiation. After the conclusion of a negotiation session, you will focus on what went well and what did not and add it to the folder you learned from your lectures.

TRACKING THE STATUS OF NEGOTIATIONS

You may have situations where the first session doesn't finish the negotiations. When this occurs, it 's critical that you chart the bargaining position. With complex deals, many distinct aspects and concessions may have to be agreed upon. You will end the talks with the understanding of where both parties are on all the issues on the table so that they are the topic of conversation at the next session.

LET THE CONTRACT FORMALIZE

When all the talks have been completed and agreed upon, it is now the time to formalize this agreement legally. The negotiated terms and conditions would usually be passed on to the legal department so that they will produce the necessary paperwork which may contain the following:

Statement or mortgage

Purchase and sale agreement (P&S)

Other types of contracts

WHY REAL ESTATE TRADING FUNCTIONS

Real estate deals will operate in a number of directions. There are lots of excellent directions to settle the agreement effectively. Unfortunately, there are also plenty of bad ways to head through a bad contract. That's what we all hope to prevent as far as possible. There are also books and e-books littering across the Internet that people can download to read, and even know how to make deals and how to manage negotiations effectively.

Be careful, though, as some unscrupulous individuals in the real estate business might give off some really bad pointers and wrong ideas to close and deal with clients. There are lots of great ideas on the opposite side which can fill in over two or more books. If you look at some autobiographies and some books written by famous estate tycoons such as Celebrity Apprentice Big Boss Donald Trump and Sam Zell, you'll find that they're using various strategies and techniques when managing their assets. Here are some tips you can use if you are an agent or broker to conclude real estate negotiations or deals with success:

Hear them out-letting the person you are dealing with speak first is important, and hearing them out is more important if you want to conclude any and all real estate negotiations successfully. Listening gives you plenty of clues and hints about what they really want and helps you gauge what counter you can offer.

Information is important-Doing your homework before a particular meeting can lead to real estate negotiations or break them. It wouldn't kill you looking into the client's likes and dislikes, the middle man and all the other people from the other side of the deal involved. Ask any successful real estate agent, and they'll tell you they can do wonders to get the good side of the clients.

The Power of Persuasion-persuasion is a powerful tool that real estate agents who want to make it big in the future need to use. The power of persuasion is something that cannot be understood immediately and perfected. This needs a lot of preparation and a lot of research. You will realize that if you find that people do what you want without knowing that it is what you want, you are the forces of persuasion who will play a major role in achieving your aim and position, you have become an effective persuader successfully.

Be Tough-Often being rough at a meeting is one of the toughest things to do. That is because certain aspects may not be in your favor, but are certainly beneficial to the other side. Sure, you can go and give in to any of these demands, but there's certainly a line in the sand that shouldn't be crossed. It will be a good idea to make them hate the possibility of having a better compromise while compromising with the opposing side, particularly whether it would cost them money or if they are going to fail. Negotiation is, as you can see, art, and you are the creator. And like any kind of art, it requires a lot of learning, experience, and skills to become the best artist in the industry that is as thriving and as old as the very civilization.

FINANCING FOR REAL ESTATE INVESTOR

Real estate investor finance will help you overcome the dangerous and more frequently than not common problem that cripples most business operations — lack of adequate start-up capital and lack of cash flow For real estate; typically there are two types of loans — conventional loans — the one you get from the bank or credit union to buy your live-in property. The other form of loan is the consumer loan, which is not the mainstream as it is typically in the finance sector for investors. Investors have a couple of options when it comes to financing their deals. They 're able to go out and get what's called private money loans. This is the funds you can borrow from private borrowers to fund your assets and restore them. Typical borrowers for this form of funding by real estate developers include family members, relatives, other creditors, and others with deep pockets in daily life. Some individuals do not receive a decent return on investment in their savings accounts, mutual plans, or any other financial asset which they know. When you can show and persuade these people that investing their money in a piece of property is a safer choice for them, they'll help you solve the all too real 'financing problem' that many potential investors face. They will finance the transactions without entering into a traditional bank at all. The financing of real estate investors, depending on the lender, is referred to by different names. When you deal with a professional investment company, it could be called a hard money loan or an equity loan. The principle is the same depending on the amount of equity you have in the contract; you get sponsored. And since it's a short-term loan, and it's such a flexible form of financing, interest rates are usually higher than conventional real estate loans.

The other major difference between a conventional loan and investor loans is the qualification criteria and guidelines for lending. You have to have good credit with a conventional loan, and you have to be able to show proof of income. The interest rate on a traditional loan is much lower, so you can repay the debt for a longer period of time. Typically the credit is not a problem in equity lending loans. You don't actually have to provide proof of employment because it's known that you're in the real estate investment business. In addition, real estate investor lending loans are typically made for less than a year, and you get approved based on the equity of the contract. Investor financing loans are worth having if you want to take your business to the next level. They 're easy; they let you easily buy properties and earn. You really ought to embrace them in your real estate investing toolkit.

FINANCING REAL ESTATE PROJECTS

So, you have made the calls, braved the weather, and went out in search of the opportunity to look at the property, and now you have it. The next step is to determine which method you will use to finance the real estate investment. This relies on a few factors like whether you want to hang onto the house or easily resell this, or how much cash you put in the contract, and how much you invest. Depends on the look of the account. Want to pay interest on a monthly basis, or do you want to pay on the back-end. Will you have to use the currency or the currency from someone else? All of that depends on your plan and on your personal wealth. Financing of real estate investments can take many forms.

MONEY FINANCE

You can get a loan from a bank or mortgage lender if you have the collateral and the requisite down payment. When following this path, it is important to ensure that you are factoring in monthly costs such as taxes and insurance and to ensure that your budget meets the monthly notice. Six months of income-free mortgages will rob off all of your benefits and leave you to work for nothing. If you buy rehab-grade property, the bank may get picky because, after all, the property will be their collateral. They might not like the idea of financing an unreasonably inhabitable property. Banks need to keep in mind that you will pay a higher interest rate on non-owner loans.

MONEY

Cold, hard cash is King when buying below market value properties. The secret to purchasing distressed property or otherwise untouchable properties is the ability to act quickly and not wait for bank approvals. If you don't have your own cash for the contract, you can use a loan of hard money. Hard money lenders will most likely be small developers, but in the hard money industry, there are some mid-size businesses. Most will bill nearly doubling a bank's interest rate, with extra points to support the offer. Most hard money lenders are seasoned real estate investors who have branched out and are going to understand better the process than most banks do. They 're going to care less about your reputation than if you have a good deal or not. Hard money lenders are only going to do business with you if you buy the property at or below 65-70 percent of the value after repair. Another way is to find your own private creditors and bring up the capital and split the profits at the tail end. Offer the lender the 1st position as leverage on the house. In that way, both private developers and hard money borrowers will theoretically make more money by foreclosing and finishing the investment themselves if you default.

CREATIVE FINANCING

Many real estate investors are specialized in purchasing homes with little or no down money. They achieve it by a variety of ways that fall under the "Creative Deals" umbrella. Typically, these are cases in which the sellers are in trouble because of foreclosure, bankruptcy, divorce, or other circumstances that cause pressure to sell quickly. Options like the Lease-Option, where the land is rented with the right to purchase later. You can deal with the current mortgage. The owner of the property will actually leave you in certain cases in return for collecting payments. Make sure that you have a professional real estate solicitor by your side for innovative offers to ensure that you do it properly and that both involved are well advised of their rights. All of these strategies will allow you to fund or gain ownership of the property, and you can then apply your wealth plan, whether it's renting out or reselling.

THE 4 TYPES OF IMMOVABLE FINANCING

For all the different types of loans and equity funding options available to borrowers these days, it's important to get a clear awareness of the advantages and drawbacks of each one, so you can select the most suitable financing option for your individual needs. Of course, given today's financial picture, options are more limited than they were some years ago, but a lender's definition of a "good deal" has changed. The point of this book is to describe the four most common types of financing available to real estate investors, while, of course, there are more than four ways of funding real estate investments, but we would address four here.

1. TRADITIONAL FINANCING

This form of loan is usually made by a mortgage broker or bank, and the lender may be a large bank or a quasi-government entity (Freddie Mac, Fannie Mae, etc.). The eligibility conditions for a loan are based on the actual financial status of the borrower-credit score, employment, properties, and debt. If you don't have good credit, decent income, and a tiny debt-to-income ratio (i.e., you earn a lot compared to the monthly bonds), you're definitely not going to qualify for traditional financing.

Advantages: Traditional financing benefits include low-interest rates (usually), low loan prices (or points), and long loan durations (usually at least 30 years). It's a great choice if you can apply for traditional financing.

Drawbacks: Conventional finance for borrowers has some drawbacks. Only a year or two earlier, you may have applied for a conventional "sub-prime" variance of banking, where income and equity were less of a problem; but with the sub-prime crisis (many of those lenders who default on their loans), such sub-prime opportunities have gone away. Yeah, when you have decent credit, profits, and minimal loans, these days, you're much better off not messing with trying to get conventional finance.

Traditional borrowers typically demand that a down payment of at least 20 percent be made. Although that isn't necessarily true, it can be hard to find borrower loans for less than 20 percent off these days by conventional lending. As an investor, negotiating with conventional borrowers can be challenging, who do not generally understand your business.

When it comes to appraisals and moving loans into their process, conventional borrowers take their time. It is best to give at least 21 days before agreeing and completing the deal. As a lender, you also try to incentivize the seller to consider your offer by agreeing to close quickly; this will also be difficult for conventional lending. Unless the borrower is lending (and most are) through Freddie Mac or Fannie Mae, there will be a cap on the number of loans you will get at one time. Generally, the cap is either 4 or 10 loans (depending on if it's Freddie or Fannie), and whether you're looking to be an ambitious borrower going after more than 5 or 10 assets at the same time, you're likely to run into this dilemma at any stage for conventional financing. There are no conventional loans in the program which will fund recovery expenses. If you are planning to buy a $100 K property and spend $30 K on rehabilitation costs, then $30 K will have to come out of your pocket; the lender will not put that money into the loan.

2. PORTFOLIO / LENDING TO CREDITORS

Some community banks will lend their own money (as opposed to having the funds from Freddie, Fannie, or any other major institution). Such banks usually have the freedom to make their own lending conditions and don't really have to go back to the borrowers' financial condition. Since some mortgage lenders (also known as "investment lenders") have the experience to objectively assess transactions, if they are sure that the transaction is good, they will be marginally less concerned with the investor defaulting on the debt, as they have already checked that the value of the property will meet the loan balance. Portfolio borrowers aren't in the real estate investment market, and they don't expect the borrower to default; despite that, they notice if the borrower has at least reasonable equity, good income, or cash reserves.

Benefits: The key advantage of portfolio lending, as stated, is that (sometimes) the borrower's financial conditions may be eased a bit, enabling lenders with less than great credit or low income to apply for loans. Below are a few more advantages:

Many equity borrowers will provide "recovery bonds," which will incorporate the rehabilitation costs through the bond, effectively requiring the borrower to fund the whole rehabilitation expense with the bond (with a down payment depends on the overall amount).

Portfolio loans also require less than 20 percent down payment, and 90% LTV is not uncommon.

Portfolio borrowers must check that it is a good investment the investor chooses to make. This provides the buyer with an additional layer of checks and balances as to if the offer they seek is a successful one. This can be a really positive sign for potential buyers!

Often, portfolio lenders are used to coping with investors and can close loans in 7-10 days many times, especially with investors they know and trust.

Drawbacks: Of course collateral loans also have disadvantages:

Most short-term mortgage loans — even as small as 6-12 months. Either you need to be sure that you can turn around and sell the property in that amount of time when you have short-term loans, or you need to be assured you can refinance before it expires and gets out of the debt.

In general, equity loans have higher interest rates and related "points" (credit costs). Portfolio loans are not uncommon to run from 9-14 percent interest and 2-5 percent of the total loan in upfront fees (2-5 points).

Portfolio borrowers will scrutinize your transactions seriously because if you seek to negotiate an arrangement that the interest is clear to you, but not to your investor, you can find yourself in a position where they may not give you the money. Since portfolio borrowers often know almost as much about the offer as the borrower, they also want to ensure if the borrower has real estate expertise. When you go to a non-experienced provider, you can find that you pay higher fees, more points, or have extra personal assurances. Once you prove to the lender by selling a couple of houses and repaying a couple of loans, things are going to get much smoother.

3. HARD MONEY

Hard money is so-named because the loan is more for the hard asset (in this case Real Estate) than for the borrower. Hard money borrowers are mostly prosperous business people (either investor themselves, or professionals like doctors and lawyers searching for a decent return on their saved cash). Hard money borrowers also don't worry about the borrower's financial status, as long as they're sure the loan can be used to fund a ton. When the deal is huge — and the borrower has the ability to perform — hard money borrowers are always likely to lend to someone with bad credit, no income, and even high debt. That being said, the poorer the borrower's financial situation, the better the offer has to be.

Benefits: The apparent advantage of hard money is that you will be able to get a loan even though you're in a very bad financial position. Again, the loan is against the deal more than the dealer is against it. And, lenders of hard money can often make quick lending decisions, providing turn-around times of just a few days on loans where necessary. Also, lenders with hard money — because they lend their own money — have the option of investing up to 100 percent of the contract, if they think it makes sense.

Drawbacks: Hard money, as you might guess, isn't necessarily the golden bullet for poor finance creditors. Since hard money is often the last resort for borrowers who are unable to apply for certain forms of loans, lenders with hard money may also place extremely high rates on their loans. Interest rates above 15 percent are not rare, and interest payments will also exceed 7-10 percent of the loan's gross value (7-10 points). This makes hard work very costly because when the offer is great, hard money will potentially eat half of the income before ever completing the sale.

4. EQUITY INVESTMENTS

Equity Investing is just a fancy word for "partner." In exchange for a set percentage of the investing and income, an equity lender will lend you money. A common scenario is for an equity investor to front all the money for a deal, but not to do any of the work. The creditor will do the job 100 percent, and both the lender and the creditor will share the income 50/50 at the top. The equity donor often gets interested in the real transaction, so sometimes the distribution isn't 50/50, but the essence of the equity fund remains the same — a party injects funds to get a share in the gain.

Benefits: The greatest advantage of an equity investor is that there are no "requirements" to be fulfilled by the borrower in order to secure the loan. When the investor opts to spend and (usually) take equivalent or greater risk than the creditor, they will do so. Sometimes, the equity donor is a relative or family member, and in the minds of all sides, the agreement is more a friendship than a lender/borrower arrangement.

Drawbacks: An equity investment has two drawbacks:

In general, equity partners are entitled to a portion of the profits, perhaps even 50 percent or more. Although the buyer usually doesn't have to pay much upfront (or even interest on the money), they'll have to fork the partner over a significant portion of the income. This may mean much less benefit than if the lender went for hard money or some other sort of high-interest loan. In the venture, equity partners would choose to play an active role. Although that may be a positive idea if the partner is seasoned and has the same dream as the donor, if not, that could be a nightmare formula.

HOUSE FLIPPING STRATEGIES

REAL ESTATE INVESTING MORTGAGE BROKERS ROLE

As an investor in real estate, it makes only sense to understand what a mortgage broker can do for you. A consultant, agent, or specialist on mortgages are all basically the same thing. Perhaps the lending cycle will come up when you buy all the cash or negotiate a bargain with the lender for 100% financing. Usually, a mortgage broker owns the business or franchise while the above work is under the mortgage broker license. Mortgage agents have access to the same mortgage products as his/her broker. When you go to a traditional bank, you are limited by the bank's offered mortgage products. If you don't meet the specific bank's loan requirements, you'll need to look elsewhere. Most investors do not know that a credit check occurs each time they go to another branch. The consequence is that every time the FICO or Beacon score passes a credit test, it goes down. This can affect the rate at which you can get or stop you from being able to qualify for a mortgage. Your FICO or Beacon score is reviewed annually by a mortgage agent and will reach 40 or more borrowers and their goods. Standard banks are limited to their own commodities only. A mortgage agent is getting the coercion out of the mortgage process. They will negotiate aggressively with lenders on your behalf. That is what they do every day.

If you are purchasing an investment property, you will be pre-qualified by a mortgage agent. Knowing how much you will apply for if this turned out to be your only financial opportunity is good. They will automate the whole lending process; secure with you the best items available and the lowest prices. They do the paperwork and give you the peace of mind that you will have the best possible solution. You will receive an explanation of the whole process, and all your questions will be answered from start to finish. It is very common to have a mortgage agent show up at your house for a 9:00 p.m. appointment for your convenience (try to get a banker to come to your house). They will provide maximum flexibility in choices on borrowing and educate you on credit and mortgage requirements. A mortgage agent is paid by the lender a finder's fee for which the mortgage has been negotiated. There's also a lending tax that the creditor pays, depending on the circumstances. In this case, a lending fee is applied, mortgage brokers do have access to benefit borrowers. The lender charges a finder's premium more often than not, and there is no trading charge. When buying an investment property, a home agent can be a perfect alley.

HOW TO GET A REAL ESTATE LOAN

Are you interested in living as an investor in real estate, but don't have the cash required to start buying investment properties immediately? If so, you certainly aren't alone. Not all real estate developers are wealthy or have infinite financial capital, given what you may personally believe—many need to turn to a financial advisor for support. Most aspiring real estate developers are seeking a deposit, usually referred to as a real estate investment deposit, before going to a finance provider. Now that you know exactly how to start a career as an investor in real estate, even if you don't have the funds you need to do this on your own, you may wonder how you can get started. As you probably already know, you will first go through the approval process if you want to get a loan from the real estate investors. This is where your best chance of obtaining a loan to invest in real estate lies.

If applying for a loan from a borrower in immovable property, you may want to consider applying for more than one lender loan. For example, you may want to think about submitting loans to some of your financial firms, like banks and credit unions, and also filling out a few applications for online loans. Since not everybody is accepted for a loan from real estate investors, multiple loan applications can improve your chances of obtaining an approval

As mentioned earlier, when looking to get accepted for a real estate investor loan, you are advised to search online lenders. It is critical that you continue with caution when turning to the online lenders. Many online scams surround lenders online. You may do want to apply for loans with well-known online lenders to maximize your odds of securing a loan from real estate investors and prevent stolen with your personal details. You may also want to seek some of the popular lending facilities. Those are the kinds of services you will apply for a loan where many internet borrowers would be able to access the application and then give you an acceptance or a rejection. It is also recommended that you, like both banks and credit unions, investigate your local financial institutions. For the most part, credit unions allow all loan applicants, including applicants in loans from real estate owners, to be members, but most banks do not have the same law. With the best chance of gaining approval for a real estate investment loan, you may want to consider applying for a loan at the bank you are a client. Most financial firms tend to lend out loans to people that are already their customers, as real estate developer loans. This doesn't mean, of course, that you can skip banks where you don't do your banking; it just means you might have more luck with your daily bank. When you want to get a loan from a real estate lender now, you are encouraged to launch the loan process right away. The faster you get approved for a loan from real estate investors, the faster you can start buying real estate investment properties, and the faster you can start making money.

GUIDELINES FOR REAL ESTATE INVESTOR REHAB LOAN

LOAN SERVICE TO BORROWERS RECOVERY

There are several services for commercial and residential real estate developers with little to no down cost to buy and rehabilitate the income-earning real estate. They are commonly considered institutional venture vehicles to make hard money loans. There could be a plan for you should you want to purchase property for investment purposes. There are basic principles for helping you decide if you are eligible for a hard money loan. The criteria that private lenders seek to lend to REI (Real Estate Investors) are in these.

Collateral-The type of property and the value of the property.

The capacity-The ability of the borrowers to make loan payments.

Money-The history of how the borrower's debts are paid.

Character-The experience as an investor and rehabber.

Assets-cash savings in case of low or other contingencies at the expense of the reconstruction.

Exit Plan-When the lender can repay the land loan.

Collateral

In case a private investor makes a hard money loan, the property form and current plus the after-recovery value are the most significant factor in. Yet, no developer needs to buy property in this industry with an endless influx of REO and troubled property. Private borrowers tend to make fast short-term loans with decent coverage and are fairly confident that they can get money back there easily.

Skills

Some funds require interest rates only over the loan term. The lender will be mindful of how the creditor has the means to fund such payments. In the past, unlike hard money loans, less focus is put on the house, and more on the willingness of the lenders to repay the loan.

Credit

Credit has become more critical in that way. The financial record demonstrates the loan reduction history and the capacity to cope with additional loans. The credit score is a statistical instrument for determining future loan repayment. Again, the lender wishes not to own the property back to their capital. Most Rehab loans currently need a minimum credit score of 680.

Character:

The character reflects the contextual aspects of a credit profile in conventional mortgage systems that help an underwriter make a decision not based on hard evidence. For Patient Recovery Loans, that will require both borrower and rehabber expertise. Many private borrowers also run criminal background checks in order to prevent possible bribery and other issues.

Assets

A creditor with a high credit score and significant assets is as secure or healthier than one with small assets when a file is underwritten for the full merits. That covers down payment and cash savings and even paying off a loan when appropriate.

Exit strategies

Now, the key part of the deal. When the borrower has a home, and plenty of collateral and a decent reputation, odds of profits and savings are strong, they will refinance the property and pay back the high-interest short-term mortgage loan from a traditional lender. This is the investor rehab lending's most important aspect, will get their money back quickly. But some private lenders can make loans to credit-scoring borrowers as small as 600 if they have a realistic exit plan and reserves to meet contingencies.

Loan to Recover

During the past, the home was perhaps the only criterion for securing a recovery loan for hard money. Today the bridge funds look at a complete file and underpin the exit strategy deals as the first priority. The days were over where credit arrived, and money didn't matter. The borrowing must apply for refinancing or have a good and verifiable way of paying off the debt by the end of the term. If that's the case, it's a victory for everyone, even the economy as a whole.

THE TOP 'LOAN SHOPPING' REAL ESTATE INVESTOR PITFALLS TO STOP

Real Estate Investment loans are the secret sauce of virtually any successful lender, beyond doubt. You may also use them to develop your real estate empire. Yet you do need to clear a few pits. For example, don't just go out there and borrow money to borrow. Obtaining a loan definitely goes a long way towards greasing the entire cycle of investing in real estate, but you have to have a plan.

Rule 1-you have to be specific about what you want the property to do before you can put it into a contract. Otherwise, you risk paying high monthly mortgages with high interest in the sky with no end in sight. Now, just the first step is to choose your exit strategy. The second fatal trap for real estate investment loans you want to stop is choosing the wrong investing plan in itself. You don't want to get a loan to invest in a house in the expectation that you can repair it and then rent it out before you can secure the bank's traditional letter of pre-approval. In other words, obtaining a real estate investment loan with an escape plan of "buy and keep" is foolish because you're not confident you will be able to secure a bank loan for over 30 years. You face getting trapped with a high-interest loan or making the home foreclosed on even worse. The last dangerous pit you want to stop is simply shopping around for a strict interest rate-based real estate investment loan.

It may be the traditional way to search for your house mortgage, but when it comes to an investment property loan, you want to be sure that you have an 'investor-friendly.' For example, you might ask your Broker if they lend on an investment property with zero down payment. Some don't, but some do so give it a suggestion you are looking for. Always search to see if they will be able to lend without maintenance payments when you repair the house. This would go a long way in making the project initiative successful. So, there you got it, the top 3 errors to look out for when you're shopping for a real estate investment loan. Consider it a point to plan your escape strategy and make it a point to look around for terms as well as favorable interest rates on your land investment loan.

Creating a Real Estate Management Company- Right Recruiting

Jobs... That's what we all need to see economies grow; so, what happens if people working for a job don't turn up until they've been working for work? If you're just starting out as an investor in real estate, your real estate company may feel like a revolving door, but take heart; the learning curve will pass. Here are a few tips and recommendations to make this step simpler, while making the construction experience more satisfying and enjoyable — the way it should be.

A Common Challenge

At some point in time, each real estate developer faced the task of building a successful investment team in any given market. If the team leader is a real estate broker, a real estate consultant, a landowner, or a project manager, it just takes the best mix of dedication and perseverance on behalf of everybody on the team. When a team member is not 100% on the same page, it reflects by their unmotivated actions, and then it impacts the team by slowing it down. With the most committed buyers, usually, those buyers who realize that the real estate is in their blood, they know it's only a matter of time before they meet the right candidates to fill the key positions on the investing team. For investors who are new and who do not want to learn how to lead teams effectively, they may give up after encountering the first one or two "bad apples." In general, hiring and managing investment teams requires a lot of patience, as well as the ability to keep communication open, honest, and solution-based.

STRATEGIES TO SURMOUNT CHALLENGES

Here are three ideas for handling the challenge of finding the right people for your investment team in real estate.

Realize the interview process is just the beginning.

We recruit people in an ideal world, and they're still a good match for the job. However, in the real world, the true character and work ethic of a person does not come through until after a while of working with them. This might be after the first or two deals if they make it to a deal. This would be a smart idea to set up a testing phase to handle the volatility of this process and recognize that the recruiting process is exactly like the procedure. A process cannot be rushed; it should be handled primarily to reduce time and energy lost. A good member of the investment team recognizes this and has the patience to work through the "thick-and-thin" of developing long-term partnerships to build riches. Only when you have genuinely good people in your team will your real estate business grow to the next level.

Going in with expectations in check - Establishing realistic expectations.

Real estate is not easy, nor is it glamourous. The daily work of sifting through countless properties in constant search for financially feasible properties requires a non-stop commitment, tenacious perseverance, and determination to get things done when they are supposed to be done. It is what it takes to keep decent offers in endless supply. As a wholesaler, rehabber, landlord, or lease-optioned, having a steady stream of financially viable assets is at the core of becoming a good real estate investor. With expectations in order and an understanding that not all characteristics are suited to the role they are expected to fill, that might create a cultural change required to embrace an attitude that can support and maintain the cycle of team bonding in a meaningful way in the long term.

Watch out for signs of incompatibility behavior.

Non-responsiveness, slow or short-sighted behavior is a red flag. Seeking to identify the problems that could impede a team leader from doing their job successfully is often the safest first step, but if the problem appears to be a concern, then a decision must be taken. The right way forward typically determines the decision, and the decision might be to let the team member go — whether they've been asked to do so or volunteer. In the conditions, when people can't connect and work together on the challenges, they can't even work together effectively; so when people are on the same page, goals are reasonable, and everybody is dedicated to building together a good real estate sector this is when a company hits the next stage of growth, and growth is what we need to fuel our own economies.

REAL ESTATE TEAM

In this big and bold information age, you would be hard-pressed to name any business that operates from start to finish with one individual. Not even an artist or author works alone. They purchase key materials made by others. They do research and gain inspiration from others. It's no different with making sure you have a great real estate team. Your team is actually far more important than the latter examples. That's why the first step to investing in real estate is the team assembly. We will explain the four key figures you need to have for your real estate team. Read on...

Attorney

The first thing to do with your attorney is to use him/her to build your business. You need to know what type of company you want to set up first, and the pros and cons of the various types of business. Your solicitor will advise and also do all that for you, from limited liability to the different types of companies and even associations. The creation of a different legal entity by forming a company is very important to you. That eliminates your personal financial state or at least limits it if something bad happens with your ventures.

Accountant

Another key component of your new real estate team is the accountants. If you don't have an accounting degree or are a math whiz, then you need one. They will crunch all the numbers. Have them make all of the financial statements and taxes. A very helpful team member that will save you loads of time on paperwork.

Broker

This person is your go-to guy in locating property and evaluating the business in which you are operating. When you want to invest in more than one spot, then one for each market is required. You'll want to send them information about what type of properties you 're looking for, and when they find candidates, they will contact you. You'll then go back with them and assess the estate.

Real Estate Director

The property manager is also a vital member of the real estate department. When you've picked and bought a piece of real estate, these guys go in and run it for you. You don't have to get them if you like, so that will save you expenses. In exchange, you 're going to have to give yourself time to do what they do: deal with renters, housing issues, maintenance, etc. Eventually, as your portfolio grows, you 're going to need to hire property managers because you're not going to have the hours to handle these things. You 're going to be too late at relaxing and cash counting. Though there are more people to be included in your real estate team from time to time, these four are what we consider to be the top-level members. The ones who you are going to have again and again. Remember to choose these people wisely because the better you choose, the better it will be for your team and business.

WHY REAL ESTATE ATTORNEY IS THE IMPORTANT MEMBER OF THE REAL ESTATE TEAM?

In order to complete the real-estate deals, you need to do a lot of paperwork. Paperwork for all real estate jobs is absolutely essential. Will you know how to finish this paperwork? Oh, the first action is taken by the real estate agent, who reveals the house to the buyer. You will be curious to discover that about 90 percent of the real estate deal is being done by the real estate agents. You will hardly find any property deal that doesn't include the real estate agent. There are, however, many other players involved in the real estate as well. The estate agents are still the favorites, however. Similarly, real-estate lawyers also play a significant role. We can't really imagine how stressful these relations with the estate are.

Many people, once in their lifetime, do real estate deals. Afterward, they hardly go for any other real-estate deals. Therefore, most of them do not have proper real estate knowledge. That is why the estate agents and the lawyers are needed. It's true the real estate agent is the busiest member of the team. You can't really discard the real estate lawyer, though. You are actually looking at the mortal combination of the estate agent and the estate attorneys. They are both very active throughout the entire process, and without them, you can't hope for the deal. Some of the lawyers and the estate agents are so seasoned that they can negotiate the deal and finish it within a day, and that's the case. The prosecutor files all the papers. The benefit in handling the documents, though, will go to the estate brokers who are responsible for finalizing both the buyer's and sellers' specifications. They note down all of the requirements while meeting buyers and sellers. They provide the relevant details to the lawyers who are experts in the preparation of the agreements, and they dare to conclude these agreements within a few days.

Working with a Team is always a good idea. You get to speak with the rest of the team members about your thoughts and think about any changes that help the business better over others. You'll also learn more about handling those circumstances and certain people's advice. The exact same law extends to the real estate market. It can't be denied, though, that if you deal with other real estate agents, some problems may arise. There are instances where others may show a low level of performance. When you're the leader, you like your subordinates to have that respect too. Prepare to treat it with patience while you know there are things to address.

HOW DO YOU WORK WITH THE BROKERS?

Team management reveals the person in you. This means that you are there to listen to everybody to see through the real core of the problem. If you do not have the reason to do so, don't simply presume and suspect one. The following should be done to handle issues between the real estate agents:

Don't ignore the problem. No matter how small or large the issue is, you always have to tackle it. Ignoring the question would only encourage the offenders to believe you don't have the courage to challenge them. That will lead to a worsening condition. Only those who admire you can not give what is because of you as a manager anymore.

Double expectations; it's a no-no. For your best performers, you can still have the heart. This means that if these individuals are upset, you can forgo the penalty. Well, you should never act that way, or it will demoralize the rest of your brokers.

Using approaches according to the attitude of the person. Perhaps, when you use the decision you used in the past, you struggle to see beyond the true heart of the issue. Which means you ought to enforce the same rules on all brokers in your squad and apply the same penalties. Okay, because there are different attitudes in the office, the fact is, penalties will be issued based on the person's personality.

Don't answer based on intuition. The superficial decision is only going to create more issues. When you want to fix problems with poor real estate prices, you need to see what induces the person not to work in the same fashion as other real estate agents. Personal concerns may arise, which leads to poor performance.

Get rid of that person if need be. When the worst happens when a person sometimes creates issues in the office, you have no alternative but to terminate his services. Yet make sure you don't do these things solely on hearsay.

When you wish to reach better revenue efficiency with your real estate business, you still have to fix challenges that arise at the office. Don't hesitate to discuss these issues. Even if you're the boss, take some time out for listening.

REAL ESTATE: RENEW YOUR PROPERTY

Weigh each renovation against its expense, its expected value, and its rental and tenant impact. You could opt for a full redesign. This amounts to paying up to 10 percent of the worth of the suites by upgrading the kitchen and bathrooms. Again, the higher your house's inherent value, the better your return. This is surely not the time to spend unnecessarily in these fields. When you buy a rental home, add in renovation and upkeep at least 2-5 percent of your gross income.

Fix some rotted wood and spackle and brick rotting, then paint them with a contemporary light, preferably a neutral tone.

Replace the front door handle with a modern, sturdy handle. When you've got an old doorbell, try replacing it with one that looks sexy.

Look to the roof. Get it checked, and have three quotations for the patch. If the roof needs maintenance, do it first, as the maintenance is filthy, and the walls can be scratched or scuffed.

Landscape

Hire a landscaper, and make adjustments easily. Replace old shrubbery and trees, clean flower beds, repair fences, paint retaining walls, fix sidewalks, and replace new, vibrant landscaping with everything. If the roots of the mature tree damage the drain and waterline cut down the branch. Otherwise, just trim the tall trees, especially if they block any windows.

Trim the branches underneath to raise the canopy. Your house will look great, you will get more light into your home, and your guests will get a better view.

Find a name change on some signs. Post a contest on your blog or view a list of names of buildings in your town. You can rent the tag, or buy it. Don't opt for the cheapest sign. Help this one stand out.

Your sign should be visible from a half-block away, at least. Attach a sign at the gate and a large upright sign at the gate of each driveway, in addition to the sign for the house.

Decks & Coats

Both decks and railings are checked. If they deteriorate or become loose, repair them immediately after you have repaired the roof. You want a secure, all-weather material covered deck surface.

Upgrade railings to the contemporary design of glass or spindle. Watch the expense as railings can be very expensive though.

A lot of parking

If your property's parking lot is packed in snow, take some summer pictures. Let the contractor look the lot and the pictures physically. Repair potholes.

Reseal and repaint lines and straighten tire stops in concrete. Tenants will complain to you and other tenants about the parking issues. Just one measure alone will alleviate tons of gripes and grievances.

Drains & Down springs

Fix all gutters, downspouts, and sinks to stop spills, sewage pollution, and sewage pooling. Ensure proper slope of the lot and extend downstream drains throughout the landscaping via weeping tile or concrete troughs. Ensure that the land runs off the water.

Coverings for Window

Both gates, doors, and blinds are replaced. Rather than being replaced, they can be repaired. Seal and cover all windows, remove any missing screens and repair window slides, and crank mechanisms so that the windows are easy to unlock.

Your manager can install coverings for the windows or supervise the task. Bedsheets and towels for large baths are not acceptable window coverings.

Outside Lighting

Make sure the outside is well-lit for visibility and to deter criminality. Activate all the lighting you want to join. Since potential buyers can drive by the building late in the evening or early in the morning, using solar-powered lights along the walkway, sidewalk, or driveway to accentuate the house. Attach your Street Address below the signs. Put a new sign in. Using energy-saving lamps or robotic photocells to turn on and off the lights.

Indoor Renovations

The design for a house can be a huge expense if you own an older B home. Including the roof, the HVAC systems, water heaters, fixtures, lamps, and all floor coverings and cabinetry need to be fixed or replaced. This is just a brief description of multi-family buildings and their investments. Study other books / courses-meet other investors who are involved in this investment area. Join a local trading club for real estate online and enter a group to address multi-family housing. There are hundreds of available tools-take advantage of them.

STARTING A PLAN FOR HOUSE RENOVATION

If you find a sort of household development either by taking on the project yourself or by using an accomplished construction company, 5 random but very useful tips are listed below on lots of different areas of the construction and design process.

1. If it comes to some change in your home, first try renovating your bathroom or kitchen. These are two of the best ways to add the most value to your home. When necessary, consider even installing an additional bathroom because this is continuously an ideal way to improve the property's worth.

2. When hiring a building contractor to perform a redesign or refurbishment of a house, make sure to be explicit about just what you intend for the entire project from the outset, and stick to that strategy. Changing the original plan continuously can easily slow down the renovation and discourage your contractor from executing without restraint. Constantly changing renovations can also result in a strained relationship between you and your trading team or the construction company's owner.

3. If the construction is finished on your house renovation, never make the final deposit until you're absolutely satisfied with the work completed. You should also make "production fees," which demands that

the contractor be given small amounts of money in some stages in the process of the work. Just keep in mind, don't settle for work that doesn't please you absolutely.

4. If plumbing is involved in your home improvement project, always have a good plan to bring water to the household or use the lavatory. It is not always easy to grasp how long it will take for a brand-new sink to be built or a plumbing project completed. And if you think that every water system operates at the end of the day, it could end up being done and have a contingency plan available just in the event. Without these basics, you definitely wouldn't want to leave your family members.

4. If you require additional space in your bathroom, you are aware that the bath and the sink will be the two factors that take up an excessive amount of space. It might be a very good idea to opt to add a pedestal sink in a small bathroom, as an alternative to one with cabinets at the base. It not only offers a chic visual appeal to a bathroom but can also bring some much-needed space back at the same time.

Yeah, you got my weird but helpful ideas there. Truly good luck with the task, and try to remember that if you have any doubts about your ability to perform any part of the project, bring in a professional company to help.

REAL ESTATE MARKETING TOOLS

Apart from the well-known bandit signs and billboard posters, there are also more conventional real estate publicity strategies that still operate for a number of business professionals. While online real estate marketing already rakes and leads in most real estate transactions, it is stupid to disregard other channels that tend to produce buyers and income for some of the world's most successful real estate brokers and businesses. Seven Offline Marketing Methods You Can Use:

1. Host Meeting Broker. This will help you network the things that matter most to the people in your industry. This is a perfect way to have an ear to the ground to maybe get suggestions for your blog, plug gaps in your marketing strategy, and perhaps come to an understanding with peers who may attract clients you like, but they don't have much need for that.

2. Press Media. Be sure to spend only in professional designs and printing services, a standard-bearing staple of offline real estate marketing resources! Stick to the basics here: research papers, white papers, explanations of goods, brochures, publicity content, etc. Whatever gets your message out there and continues to scream it once your client gets it home and reads it.

3. Support local and charitable organizations. There are tons of ways to give back to the community, from sponsoring a local baseball team to taking a highway. This will not only create you as a cornerstone of the society but will make your name identifiable immediately. This comes into play when friends or relatives of a community leader are searching for an immovable entity in the area-guess whose name is at the tip of their tongues? Be sure you're careful and prefer organizations that suit your mission and beliefs.

4. Releases to Press. The target here is double. First, you want to get detailed press releases setting up your real estate agent as the local "go-to" service. Such updates will be timely, well documented, and cover all of the area's current developments and breaking news. It will draw the interest of news and program managers at your local radio stations, prompting them to contact you on matters which require your expertise. These are the kinds of media appearances that would make the agency a household name, increasing customer trust, and improving revenue and referrals.

4. Keep Real Estate workshops free of charge. Making speeches included teaching prospective real estate buyers how to reach the market, or telling people how to get the most resale value added to their house. Speak about things that people will profit from-give them "the get" as in "what do they get to attend?" Instead, focus on the get. Don't sell your services, set up an authority, and be helpful come back to you ten times.

6. Catchy Card Company. Business cards will cause you to stand out or get tossed out-it's up to you which name you want to put on paper. Drop-cards, for starters, are a fun way of receiving attention. These look like folded up money bills, which at least leads people to pick them up and look at them. We equate with putting money in their wallet when they see the face and are left with a positive feeling. Throw them in places where they can be found by men. Or how about a business card folding up to a house? Do you have a business card that is clear white? That's great for them to write a phone number to someone else and then throw it when they're done with it.

7. Vehicle Wraps. Every day you drive through your town or city, hundreds and thousands of people walk by. Let your car bundled with the logo or the logo and face of the real estate firm. Let people know everywhere you go, who you are. It's a one-time and super successful cost to get you recognized as a resident of the city, not just a name on a sign in front of a house. The combination of these offline marketing methods with online marketing strategies is the true secret to real estate growth.

CONCLUSION

In the first place, if you want to be successful in investing in real estate, you have to understand that investing in real estate is a business, and you become the CEO of that business. It is also important to build the right perspective on investment real estate as the first line of business and to be able to differentiate between purchasing a home and investing in real estate."You purchase a house to stay and raise a family; you purchase an investment property to pay for your mortgage, live comfortably, and raise your family in style". In other words, to invest effectively in real estate, you have to recognize that it is not curb appeal, facilities, floor plan, or location that will turn you on or off the invention. A straightforward collection of priorities that outlines your investment plan is one of the most critical aspects of successful investing. Remain, realist. Yeah, we all hope to make millions of monies off our real estate investment properties, but dreaming isn't the same as voicing concrete expectations and a plan for achieving them. Here are some recommendations: What amount of cash can you comfortably invest? Whose yield levels do you intend to generate? Are you hoping for quick cash flow, trying to make money when the property is resold, or simply looking to get tax shelter benefits? How long are you considering owning the property? Which sum of your own money can you afford to commit to managing the day-to-day property operations? Which future net worth do you expect to achieve by savings, and by when? Which kind of profit property do you feel more secure, residential, or commercial possession, or does that matter?

As a novice to real estate investment, you probably know little about income property in your local market. Do a market analysis and know as best as you can about your area's income levels, wages, and rates of occupation. The more you are prepared, the more often you can notice a good (or bad) offer when you look at it. Calculating the cash balance, rate of return, and property productivity is important for a profitable investment sector in real estate. As CEO, you have to know what you are getting, particularly if you're trying to find out which of many investment opportunities will be the most lucrative. You've got two options: Invest in tech for the investment in real estate. This will help you discover the cash flow and return values of the rental property and generate your own analytical reports. Plus, you gain a broader understanding of investment nuances in real estate by running the numbers yourself. In turn, you may be less likely to fall victim to somebody's wiles with little concern about how you're spending your money. Consult for someone who owns systems for real estate investing and is willing to manage, show, and address the figures.

Getting to know a knowledgeable specialist is a perfect way for newcomers to get involved with an investment property as an astute expert will expose you to local market trends, suggest a property that fulfills your investment goals, and address strengths and disadvantages regarding the property's actual results. However, just be sure to work with an immovable person who understands real estate investment property. Make sure the agent has a strong grip on key financial metrics inherent in real estate investing, understands how to calculate productivity and rate of return, has the capacity to provide the data you need to make wise investment choices and, most significantly, displays a sincere interest in how you spend your money. The last thing you want to do is to be associated with an agent who will dump you under the bus just to receive a reward. Ask about cap rate, cash-on-cash return, and then request an APOD or Proforma Income Statement. If they stand there looking at you like a deer into the headlights of a car in response to even these basics, find another agent. Start Investing. YES, that's it. It's time for you to get started. Here's to your real estate investing success.

www.ingramcontent.com/pod-product-compliance
Lightning Source LLC
Chambersburg PA
CBHW052358220526
45465CB00003BB/1155